THE MEANDERING RIVER OF UNFATHOMABLE JOY

Finding God and Gratitude in India

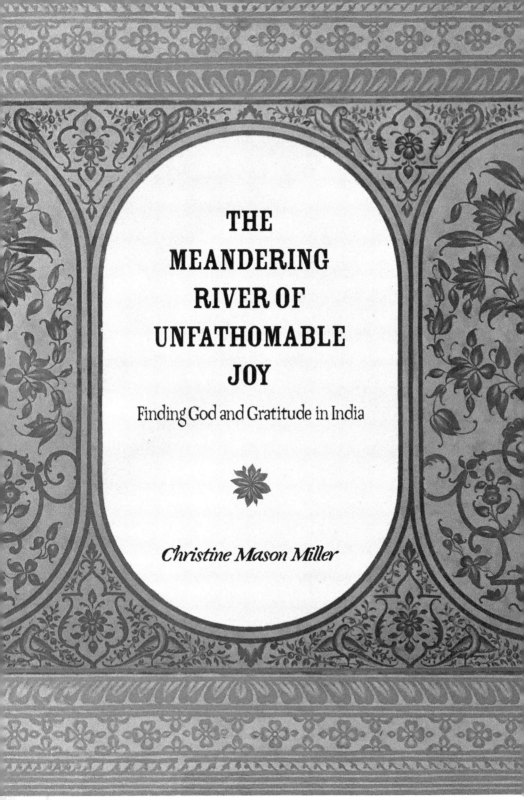

THE
MEANDERING
RIVER OF
UNFATHOMABLE
JOY

Finding God and Gratitude in India

✦

Christine Mason Miller

For L.E.D.

FOUR ANNAS

HIS HIGHNESS SIKANDAR-SAULAT IFTIKHAR-UL-MULK
BHOPAL STATE
NAWAB MOHAMMAD HAMIDULLAH KHAN

چار آنے

TABLE OF CONTENTS

FOREWORD

We think of the word *pilgrim* most commonly as a noun: a person who takes a journey for religious reasons. As a verb, *to pilgrim* means to travel, to wander, to seek out what the soul treasures in an unexplored land. A pilgrimage to a sacred site holds the possibility of spiritual redemption and inspiration for living one's life more closely connected to the Source of All Things.

Spirit lives inside the constructs of chaos, just as it exists on a newborn baby's sleeping face. The two are neither separate nor contradictory. Safety and sanitary conditions do not guarantee one's connection to something greater. God's presence tends to be detected when we are at our most vulnerable—when sick, poor, at the rock-bottom crossroads in life, where darkness is found in light and light is found in darkness. To seek the in-between spaces that hold both as sacred is the purpose of pilgriming. This dual inhabitance is the essence of spiritual growth and transformation.

I've heard many travelers say upon their return from India that they "have no words." Although I have never been there, this does not surprise me. What language can possibly describe a golden journey of the soul that hinges on delight in paradox? Profound experiences cannot easily be relayed with the element of precision we would most enjoy. Those tending to life back at home can only subsist on a colorful buffet of photographs while the real flavor and texture of India's nourishment remains tucked into the wordless heart of the deeply nourished pilgrim.

Several years ago, I traveled to the rural, magical countrysides of England with Christine to visit the sacred sites of Avalon. The discomforts weren't nearly what are detailed in this book, but the gems of the adventure—as well as the space out of time in a foreign land, arm-in-arm with beloved sisters—are like a medal emblazoned across my heart. Her dailies from India provide a glimpse into a mystical place from her perspective—as a tall, blonde woman sticking out as an obvious tourist, her expressions curious and open in the same way they've been when she traveled through places like Jordan, Japan, and Cuba. What I know of Christine is that wherever she goes, whether near or far, she takes in every detail and nuance, honoring every experience, environment, and circumstance that exists outside her usual range of motion.

To pilgrim is to journey outward into unknown places with a fresh and open heart in order to bring the stories, wisdom, and lessons back to the home hearth for integration. Christine's travel diaries allow the reader to sample the saffron, finger the silk, and sip from the holy waters where life and death are equally drenched and immersed in gratitude.

Pixie Lighthorse

Evening on the Ganges

INTRODUCTION

The first stamp in my passport was affixed by a customs agent in Paris when I was twenty-two years old. After spending the previous four years studying all the highlights of European art and architecture as an art student, my first order of business upon graduation was to go see them. The plan was for a six-week backpacking adventure with my best friend, where we had to figure out train schedules, subway maps, and currency exchange rates while subsisting on baguettes, water, and not much else. We stayed in youth hostels, slept on trains, and climbed the narrow, winding steps to the top of Il Duomo in Florence, all on less than fifty dollars a day.

More than two decades later, I traveled to India, twice. I worked with a travel agent on both occasions who arranged for everything ahead of time—hotel reservations, restaurant options, private tour guides, and a driver. There was very little my travel companions or I had to figure out or decipher on our own. And since our travel agent had an office in India, we had a local contact who was always available if there was a problem.

Despite all of these amenities and conveniences, India still manages to be the most challenging, intriguing, and engaging place I've ever visited. I've gotten lost in Buenos Aires, trekked through a jungle in Australia, danced on a rooftop in Havana, and floated in the Dead Sea—experiences that made me feel wide awake to the miracle of being alive and able to explore different parts of this planet. I've experienced discomfort and homesickness on every trip I've taken, but in India everything is amplified and fractalized like a three-dimensional kaleidoscope. Whatever is happening in India, and whatever kind of reaction I am having to it, I receive it and experience it as if my entire body is transparent and porous—for India demands that every molecule and moment be wholly absorbed. "Otherwise," India seems to say, "what's the point?"

There is something about India—home to Bollywood, the Taj Mahal, and Gandhi—that inspires its own kind of fascination. After traveling to far-flung places like Cuba, Japan, and Jordan, the stamp in my passport that gets the most wide-eyed wows is India. Most everyone wants to know about the crowds, the noise, and the pollution. When I confirm all of those things are, indeed, overwhelming, the next question is *why*—as in, "Why did you want to go back a second time?"

In most people's minds, India is exotic in a disquieting way. The curiosity people have about it exists at arm's length; they are interested in learning about India because they are certain they never want to go there.

India is not an easy place to describe beyond what is visible to the naked eye, and my experiences there defy categorization. Every time I try to explain why I was eager to return after my first visit, even though I'd gotten sick and came home thoroughly exhausted, I find myself fumbling over words. I have yet to find a narrative that concisely summarizes the allure India holds for me. How do I explain how close I came to God in India without making it sound cliché or corny or mawkish? It's like asking me to describe the tiny burst of joy I feel in my bones every time my husband says my name. Both are precious moments in my life, and both are impossible to articulate.

In a relatively brief amount of time, India slipped into my heart and took up permanent residence, not merely because of the foreignness of it or the wildness of it but because of the way her complicated web of humanity provided a glimpse of God at work. In situations both mundane and extraordinary, India challenged me to be fully present, to surrender to each moment, and to take it all in. She encouraged me to pay attention to everything around me and to what was happening within me, guiding me toward prayer and stillness everywhere I went. She provided examples of faith and spirituality in action around every corner and inspired in me a desire to know more about where certain rituals came from and what they mean in the twenty-first century.

I found a million reasons to feel gratitude in India. Within the pages of this book are a few of the stories that inspired that gratitude. It is part diary, part encyclopedia, part visual journal, part philosophical reflection. It is emotion and thought, heart and mind. It is a thank-you card to India and a love letter to God, an exploration of the way so many moments, mishaps, and joyful surprises helped me discover new ways of tapping into and expressing my faith.

Will this book inspire you to want to visit India? Maybe; maybe not. Like any journey—physical, geographical, psychological, relational, or spiritual—the longing has to come from deep within. Such a yearning might make itself known early in life; other times it waits for the right kind of ignition to light the spark. Whether this book wakes up in you a newfound desire to experience India for yourself or affirms your decision not to go there, I hope, at the very least, it shines a light on your spiritual path and unearths something you've always known was inside of you, some tiny jewel of awareness about your brilliant uniqueness and your connection to what is ineffable, sacred, and the source of all life.

Going to India isn't a prerequisite for growing more fully into your skin or deepening your relationship with God. At any moment, no matter what is happening, only one word is needed to relax into the flow of all that was, is, and will be: *Yes*. Yes, I am here. Yes, I surrender. Yes to my strength, and yes to my heart. Yes to every single thing.

May 2018
Milwaukee, Wisconsin

INDIA BY THE NUMBERS

Population: 1.2 billion
Seventh largest country by area
Second most populous country
Sixth largest economy
29 states
23 official languages

Languages:

Assames

Bengali
Bodo
Dogri

English
Gujarati

Hindi
Kannada

Kashmiri
Konkani

Maithili
Malayalam

Marathi
Meitei
Nepali

Odia

Punjabi

Sanskrit

Santali
Sindhi

Tamil
Telugu
Urdu

Religions:

79.8% Hindu

14.2% Islam

2.3% Christian

1.7% Sikh

.7% Buddhist

.4% Jain

.9% Other

JANUARY 9, 2018 *Preparations*

The calendar flipped to 2018 nine days ago, and now I'm on my way to India. Since I started planning this trip, my entire life has been packed up and transported from Santa Barbara, California, to Milwaukee, Wisconsin. My husband and I have been in our new house only three months, and we are still adjusting to the reality of being two thousand miles away from our nearest and dearest. This will be my first overseas flight since we moved, and it feels surreal to be taking off from Chicago's O'Hare airport today with temperatures in the teens and snow on the ground—a far cry from the palm-tree-laden landscape of my former home.

The impetus for our move was his desire to return to the place he spent his formative years. We are now residents of Wisconsin because during the forty years my husband was building a career in California and logging millions of miles on airplanes around the world, his heart was always in the same place: Milwaukee. The decision to relocate involved months of discussion and contemplation, but once we set things in motion, the universe conspired to get us on our way as quickly as possible. It seemed as if this corner of the Midwest longed for his return as much as he did.

After leaving the shiny, happy sunshine of Southern California, where I'd lived since 1995, for the wintery Midwest, I began the journey of being a bit of a stranger in a strange land. I say *a bit* because it isn't as if we've moved to Greenland, but I am still having to adjust to everything that is new—the route to the grocery store, winter clothing, and driving in the snow, not to mention figuring out how to stay close and connected to everyone we left behind in Santa Barbara.

The move has been daunting, overwhelming, and thrilling. I like to remind myself these are the same descriptors I'd use for a roller coaster ride, something I loved as a kid. I have embraced this journey as a big, bold adventure—and I am also just beginning to come down from the state of airy uprootedness I experienced for most of 2017. With each change-of-address form, packed box, and tearful goodbye, it was as if the laws of gravity, bit by bit, loosened their grip on my body until I'd lost all the routines and comforts that made me feel grounded, safe, and tethered to the earth.

It has been a surprisingly solid place for me to land during this transition—India, that is. Which feels funny to say because India is not a place I think of as particularly steady. Ever since my first visit four years ago, I've described India using words like *crazy, overwhelming*, and *complex*. I'm not going there now in search of rest and relaxation or to recover from our move. The idea of it being a stable place to land emotionally and psychologically makes me want to laugh.

I suppose it isn't India that has felt like a lifeline during this time but rather the plans and preparations that have been made to go there with my three fellow travelers—Barb, Jennette, and Kolleen, close girl-friends with whom I've traveled extensively before. I took my first trip to India in 2014 with Barb, in fact. During my recent cross-country relocation, I pinned this trip on my calendar as a known entity in the midst of all the other endless uncertainties. The steps we took to map out a two-week itinerary through four major cities and two villages became pinpoints on my calendar, with a single thread connecting them all and leading us to today—our departure date. Even knowing any number of circumstances could have derailed the trip, I've looked to this block of days as a time when I can leave behind a trail of empty moving boxes, bubble wrap, and all the people who, upon learning I've moved from Santa Barbara to Milwaukee, look at me like I am nuts.

Before we started planning our 2014 trip in earnest, Barb and I had talked a lot about our concerns, desires, and expectations. It was an exercise that essentially involved making lists of all the ways we were crazy and all the things we were afraid of. After confirming our neuroses and idiosyncrasies were pretty well matched, we came up with some basic parameters—arrangements that would ensure, as much as possible, our safety, health, and sanity.

We worked with an experienced travel agent based in India who took care of all hotel reservations and provided tour guides in every city plus our own driver, which sounds very fancy but is relatively inexpensive in India. We weren't interested in trying to decipher train schedules or in figuring out how to eat and drink safely. We knew ourselves well enough to know what would and wouldn't make for a pleasurable experience in one of the most populated—and polluted—places on earth.

The four of us have stuck to this same basic approach for this trip, which has provided an extra dose of encouragement for everyone. Barb and I have been through this process before, which has made us the *de facto* travel coaches for Jennette and Kolleen. We have been their go-to guides for all questions related to visas, vaccinations, and mosquito repellent.

Although Barb and I had been talking about taking a second trip to India ever since our first, a few details from our previous experience got me wondering early on whether or not returning, and with four people this time, was really the best idea. As our departure date grew closer and I began organizing in earnest, I kept thinking about India's air quality, which has gotten so bad that schools, airports, and construction projects were shut down in recent months. I kept thinking, too, about how sick Barb and I got on our first trip. Although we were grateful our illnesses had nothing to do with digestion, our health was severely compromised by respiratory issues that inspired deep, heaving coughs for nearly the entire trip. Our bodies could handle what we ate but struggled with the air we inhaled.

A few days ago, as I rolled up my rain jacket and tucked it in my suitcase, the more disconcerting elements of India came to mind: the feral dogs, the throngs of people, the traffic, the noise, and the poverty. I recalled a moment in Jaipur, about halfway through our trip, when I looked at Barb with teary eyes in the middle of lunch and meekly said, "I'm having a hard time."

I didn't dwell on these details, but they gave me pause. I realized that if an unexpected event of some kind had come along and prevented our trip, I wouldn't have been terribly heartbroken. It wasn't that I wished for something to go wrong; rather, I was acknowledging an unexpected level of ambivalence—a feeling I never thought I would associate with India. I looked forward to many things about this trip to India . . . and I was aware my life wouldn't be anything less if I didn't go, even though the process of planning the trip had been such a welcome and encouraging distraction during our move. Like so many moments during the transition, my head and my heart didn't feel aligned, which I've come to see as a potent reminder to trust the process.

Throughout my life, I have been shown the futility of trying to map out perfect scenarios for pretty much anything. Whatever the situation, I try to do the best I can, to move toward what I want, and to allow for the natural flow of things. In the days leading up to our trip, that flow carried a swell of mixed feelings about going to a place I love despite its complications and having to leave my home to do it. There was nothing that needed to be fixed in that scenario; the feelings weren't a sign that something was wrong. I made copies of my passport, ordered Polaroid film, and stocked up on my favorite ginger candies while letting the contradictions snuggle up together. Then I said goodbye to my husband and my dog and began a journey that is taking me halfway around the world.

Once I am settled into my seat, I pray. I pray for a safe journey and for my friends to have a safe journey. Kolleen and Barb are flying together from Los Angeles; Jennette is departing from Seattle. I pray for my husband and our dog to be safe and peaceful while I am away. I pray for my family and give thanks for all the blessings my husband and I have received during what has been the biggest transition of our sixteen-year relationship. I pray for family members going through a divorce and for friends in Santa Barbara still recovering from the Thomas Fire.

In my backpack I have a small organza bag with a few cherished items: a faceted quartz crystal; an Our Lady of Guadalupe figure; a Catholic charm in the shape of a cross; and a smooth, smoky quartz stone said to offer grounding and protection. I've also brought four tiny packets in my suitcase—gifts for my friends—each one containing dried lavender from my garden, salt, a tiny quartz crystal, and a smooth pebble. A small mandala is drawn on one side of each pebble, and a single word on the other: *love, joy, light, peace.* I know that in India, we will have countless opportunities to offer these tokens in a way that feels prayerful and holy, be it at a shrine dedicated to Ganesh, at the Yamuna River, or on the steps of a Hindu temple. This is the reason I am bringing them: so we can participate in some small way in the spiritual weavings that take place everywhere.

It is this part of India—the sacred, spiritual, prayerful side of its complicated, exuberant personality—that moved me most when I visited four years ago. Ever since then, when someone has asked me to describe my time there, I have offered the same summation: "I've never felt God's presence more viscerally than in India." When they've wanted to know what I meant by this, I've explained that somehow, in some way—a way we, as Westerners, can't quite wrap our heads around—all the living beings that crowd the streets of India are provided for. This happens in ways we are used to, and perhaps barely so. But considering the sheer numerical makeup of India, it is nothing short of miraculous that so many living beings are at least somewhat sustained there. They say God works in mysterious ways, a concept I am certain was born in India.

I have no interest in romanticizing India, in painting a picture that leaves out details like old women begging on the street or injured dogs left to fend for themselves. There is much in India that is unsettling, unnerving, and assaulting, and it is impossible to comprehend how so many aspects of India are going to evolve. If the current population of stray dogs continues to run loose and breed uncontrollably, how will this ever be managed? How can the catastrophic pollution that has damaged the Ganges River, where bathers risk emerging from the water with typhoid and hepatitis, be undone? When I say I feel God's presence on a visceral level in India, I mean I see God getting His hands dirty here in ways I've never seen anywhere else—doing the best He can in a place that is still finding its way as an independent country, free from British rule only since 1947, and as the most populated democracy in the world.

I might not be traveling around India in the company of a twenty-person tour group on a lumbering bus, but I understand my experience of it will happen, for the most part, in a bubble. But whether I see India from the vantage point of a bus, a boat, or a bicycle, it would take real effort not to see that the layers separating light from dark, life from death, and growth from decay are as thin as an onion skin in India. The juxtapositions weave their way in and out of each other in ways both mundane and spectacular, one side expanding into its fullest essence as it nestles closer to its converse twin.

This is where I feel God—in the in-between spaces of both/and, where there are no contradictions but instead a watery interplay of circumstances, struggles, experiences, and cycles that provide the fullness of the human experience. Life is made meaningful because there is death. The sun is at its most spectacular when it bursts out of the darkness at dawn. It isn't that my awareness of these truths is absent at home, that I don't feel God's presence in Milwaukee, but that in India, with so little time to recover between one situation and the next, my senses remain on high alert and are therefore awake and receptive to *everything*.

Beyond my entreaties for safety and wellness in India, this is also what I pray: for that character of awakeness unique to me in India, bringing my senses and soul alive to all the mysteries of this world and my existence. I want to go there with old questions and come home with new ones. I want to live some of the answers while I'm there.

As my plane takes off and heads into the clouds, I do the thing I know I will be able to do at any moment, no matter what awaits me in India. I turn to God, and I pray.

GANESHA

Ganesha is one of the most well-known Hindu deities, revered as the remover of obstacles. As the god of new beginnings, success, and wisdom, he is worshipped at the start of rites and ceremonies.

JANUARY 10, 2018 *Expectations*

It is mid-afternoon in Delhi, I've just arrived, and I am already comparing everything here to the memories of my arrival four years ago, which was at night. What was jarring at that time was the quiet. I expected pandemonium when I arrived at the Indira Gandhi International Airport on my first visit. Delhi is the second most populous city in the world, and everyone I knew who had been to India told me the same thing: "Get ready. India is *crazy*." Armed with antibiotics, probiotics, and two cameras, I stepped off the plane in a state of surreal wonder. Our plane had landed in a sea of wispy fog beneath a nearly full moon with very few other planes coming and going, making the airport eerily devoid of activity. As I made my way out of the gate that first time, moving through customs and toward baggage claim, I kept expecting to turn a corner and find the India of my imagination: the crowds and the chaos and the crazy. I kept expecting . . . something else.

And while it isn't necessarily noisy this time, more passengers mill about at this time of day. I make my way through the terminal and come across uniformed officials every fifty feet or so who ask me a question in hurried, choppy English. At each of these human checkpoints, I offer an affirmative nod, even though I don't know what they are saying. Eventually, one of their inquiries feels especially urgent and I stop and try to figure it out. A fellow traveler behind me assesses the situation and explains that the official is trying to determine if I am headed to another flight or if Delhi is my final destination. Once this is cleared up, I am told to go left. Around the corner, I take in a monumentally welcome sight: short lines through customs.

Kolleen, Barb, and Jennette took the same flight out of Vancouver, which landed a few minutes after mine. It doesn't take long before I find them in baggage claim. As soon as we've pulled all of our suitcases off the conveyor belt, relieved everything arrived safely, we head toward the exit.

We move through the crowds, and I smile in expectation, hopeful for a repeat performance of what happened four years ago. Back then, Barb and I walked through the final exit and faced a small crowd of people waiting for their loved ones. Immediately, a sign with the name of our travel agency sprang up out of the crowd like a jack-in-the-box, which we thought was hilarious. The bearer of the sign, who was our guide for Delhi, saw the two of us—tall, blonde, and frazzled—and didn't doubt for a second we were the ones put in his charge. It was a story Barb and I told repeatedly, which had planted a seed that made me want an encore performance.

But when we walk through the same exit now and scan the crowd, most everyone looks beyond us in search of whomever they are waiting for. When we find our tour guide a few minutes later, the travel agency sign held still in front of his chest, making it clear he was waiting for us to find him, I am reminded I am on a different adventure this time and that comparisons and expectations will only serve to disappoint.

India had plenty of other surprises—and tumult—in store for me on my first trip, as it does now, and, like before, the first ninety minutes on the ground provide me with the most abrupt and absolute shift in perspective. Whatever my preconceptions were of India in 2014, it was the magnificently unexpected lack of chaos upon my arrival that set the tone for the following seventeen days. Everything I thought I knew, wanted to believe, or had every reason to expect about my time in India was immediately called into question and snuffed out like the butt end of a cigarette. By the time Barb and I had pulled up in front of our hotel—a cozy bed-and-breakfast situated away from the city center—I knew I wasn't in India merely to live out a long-held dream of seeing this part of the world. I was there to *surrender*—to feel the current of India swell beneath me, just as I'd learned to do in the Pacific Ocean on a surfboard, and to embrace the thrill of being taken for a ride.

Today, as the four of us head to our hotel, I feel the same way.

गौ माता के दर्शन मात्र से जीवों का
रोगी, भूखी-प्यासी गायों को औषधि
हाथ से दो।
थोड़ा सा अधिकार मिला
दुनियां को तबाह कर दिया।
थोड़ा सा यश मिला
दुनियां पर हसने लगी।
दर्पण ही तोड़ डाला।
मौर्य MIX & MATCH
Manufacturers & Wholesaler
& CAK
Tasty

Evening crowds in Delhi

JANUARY 11, 2018 *Qawwali*

The journey to the Hazrat Nizamuddin Dargah in Delhi is one of trust.
Barb and I learned this in 2014 when we returned to our hotel at the end
of our first day in India and confessed to each other that just a few hours
earlier, when our tour guide was leading us down a maze of narrow,
angular alleyways toward the Sufi temple that was our destination, our
hearts felt like they were about to pound their way out of our chests.

We had made a few specific requests of our travel agent when we
planned our 2014 trip, and seeing live music—something the locals, not
just the tourists, actually listen to—was one of them. When we saw
"*Qawwali* singers" (pronounced ka-va-lee) on our itinerary, we looked
forward to experiencing an authentic expression of India's creative heart
and soul. And we got that, along with a lesson in surrender and flow.

That evening, the tour guide we'd been with all day hadn't explained how our evening would proceed; he simply introduced us to a new guide, said goodbye, and then headed off with our driver, Mr. Sanjay. Barb and I were jet-lagged but energetic, excited about the evening of live music ahead. Our new guide was slightly shorter than both of us but made steady eye contact from the moment we shook hands. After our initial pleasantries, he dove into a discussion about God and faith and all the ways both are made manifest.

Meanwhile, the procession of traffic in front of us whizzed by at a steady clip. People pushed past us on foot and two wheels in both directions. Between these two rivers of humanity, there was a dog—golden-haired, lean, about the size of a small labrador—lying down on the pavement. But it wasn't the pavement of the sidewalk; it was the road, with cars passing just a few feet away, oftentimes closer. This was a detail of the evening Barb and I commiserated over later that night—that we both zeroed in on this slumbering canine (oblivious to the danger it was in!) and then had an inordinately hard time concentrating on anything our new tour guide said.

While our guide spoke, his feet were firmly planted on the sidewalk, which meant ours were too. The unfortunate reality of this was that Barb and I had to spend the next ten to fifteen minutes doing our best to give him our attention while also trying to will the dog to move and praying it didn't get run over in the meantime.

When it finally came time to make our way to the temple, I was relieved, which felt selfish, considering the dog was going to continue to be perilously close to traffic even if I couldn't see it. We began following our guide toward a wide pedestrian area with vendors on either side while my attention lingered on my hopes for the dog's safety. But as we made our way farther down the alley, my mind wasted no time reorienting itself toward my immediate surroundings.

I don't actually know where we're going, I thought, suddenly feeling exposed to any number of potential dangers. Delhi was reeling over the news of the beating and rape of a Danish tourist that had happened days earlier, and I reminded myself to move and walk the way tour books for any part of the world instruct in the safety section of their guides: confidently, purposefully, with conviction. When our tour guide pulled us aside, inadvertently backing us into a corner, I made an immediate, firm request that we keep making our way to the temple.

Am I being paranoid? I wondered. *Is jet lag causing my mind to twist and morph the scene around me into something malevolent?* It wasn't rational to think our tour guide had any ill intentions or that our travel agent wouldn't have fully vetted him ahead of time. But I was in a foreign country, which meant I had a different kind of radar, one that has served me well across five continents and twenty-two countries. I am adventurous, yes, but alongside that sense of adventure I maintain an awareness that any time I am not in my own country, I open myself up to new vulnerabilities. My insistence that we not remain stuck in a corner as the darkness settled in was not made out of fear so much as a desire to avert potential troubles, both for Barb and me and our guide.

While following the route to the Hazrat Nizamuddin Dargah, I thought about my husband and what his reaction might be if a tiny camera were perched on my shoulder, enabling him to watch this scene unfold. I walked through a crowded, noisy labyrinth that could have been created by M. C. Escher. Alleyways became increasingly narrow, turns were more frequent, and, after a few sets of downward steps, the promenade was covered. The fading glow of the evening sky was replaced by the harsh glare of fluorescent bulbs, which lit up displays of flowers, shawls, books, religious trinkets, and tiny bottles of rose water—offerings for the temple that stood somewhere beyond the walkway.

At one inconspicuous spot, our guide instructed us to remove our shoes and deposit them alongside a few other pairs of shoes situated on a low shelf. A few guys sat nearby, but it didn't appear it was anyone's job

to pay attention to the shoes. However, our guide assured us they would
be right where we left them when we returned. When I noticed him slip a
small rupee bill into the hands of one of the men, I understood there was
a system for this and I didn't need to worry.

After depositing our shoes, we were told to cover our heads. As we
turned the corner, the walkway widened. Just beyond was our reward.

We emerged from a space that was beginning to feel slightly claus-
trophobic into an open courtyard with garlands of globe lights the size of
golf balls. Rows of them floated above our heads and were secured along
the edges of the Hershey's kiss–shaped dome that sat atop the main
temple. The temple was a squat, square structure with an open, outer
area that wrapped around the periphery of the enclosed inner temple. A
steady stream of men carrying trays full of rose petals flowed in and out
of the temple while women, who were not allowed inside, sat together in
the portico. Windows provided a glimpse into the inner temple, where I
saw marble slabs with a carved pattern of openings resembling a beehive.
Red and orange strings were tied around many of them and dangled
limply. The rest of the façade was embellished with intricate patterns of
gold, red, and green.

I took a deep breath, surveying it all. Most of the men wore simple
white caps; many had thick beards. People of all ages snapped pictures
and selfies. Everything was brightly lit, but I could still see the night sky
above.

We spent a few minutes wandering around the area and made a
short visit with the resident Sufi priest. Then our guide got us settled in
for the music. Once it began, I was transported.

Qawwali is Sufi devotional music. With roots that extend to the thir-
teenth century and a growing popularity in the twentieth century, it is
performed at the Hazrat Nizamuddin Dargah every evening. Almost

exactly four years after the evening Barb and I spent in the thrall of its mystical melodies for the first time, I am thrilled to be back in the same spot with Barb, Kolleen, and Jennette.

Now that I am familiar with the routine of getting there, I can envision all four of us moving along as if on a game board—one block takes us into the market area, four blocks to our first turn, five blocks later we deposit our shoes, and then, at the end, the temple courtyard rises up before us as if in a dream. Along the way, we pass bins filled with roses, portable metal food carts, displays of kitchenware, and the occasional goat.

We are at the end of our first full day in India, one that began at the Jama Masjid, India's largest mosque, and then took us to Chandni Chowk, a lively marketplace that has been in existence since the seventeenth century. In Delhi, shoppers looking for a variety of a particular item—say, a silk flower garland—can browse to their hearts' content in Chandni Chowk, literally translated Moonlight Square, the oldest and busiest market in Delhi.

The displays in Chandni Chowk are crowded yet meticulously organized. Rolls of fabric trimmed with shiny metallic thread and embroidered images of flowers, butterflies, and bicycles are stacked neatly so each pattern is discernible. Wide, shallow bowls filled with nuts and dried fruits are situated on tiered shelves at street level, while behind them, on the shelves lining a store's walls, more inventory is artfully displayed in large glass jars. One container isn't merely filled with dried figs; it is filled with rows of dried figs stacked vertically the length of the jar, creating an orderly pattern. We see displays of small organza bags in every color imaginable, carved wooden elephants, gold filigree jewelry, hanging garland made with plastic beads and flowers, silk fabric by the yard, small kitchen accessories, and an assortment of fried snacks and other local delicacies. Bargaining is encouraged, and it is sometimes necessary to remove one's shoes to enter a shop.

After walking through its crowded, narrow corridors, the four of us emerge with a combined stash of a few of the market's offerings. Jennette is going home with multicolored pom-pom trim, and Kolleen chose a few rolls of intricately embroidered ribbon. Barb and I stocked up on packages of chai and spices, and I couldn't resist a golf-ball-sized chunk of salt the color of pale garnet. From the market we go to lunch and then wrap up our daytime excursion with a visit to Humayun's tomb at sunset. At this time of day, the Persian-influenced structure made of white marble and red sandstone practically glows, softening the lines of everything around it.

Here at the Hazrat Nizamuddin Dargah, the courtyard is slightly more crowded than it was four years ago, and visitors are already seated on either side of the musicians' area. After some maneuvering, we settle on the far side of the courtyard from where we entered, and a young gentleman sitting next to me initiates a conversation.

I learn he is married and lives outside the city. He has never been to the United States but has family in Dallas. After our initial chit-chat, even after the music starts and despite our sitting knees to elbows with everyone around us, he continues to lean over every few minutes to share another question or tidbit about his life.

"How much does it cost to live in the US?" he wants to know.

"I want to visit the United States, but my wife doesn't," he shares matter-of-factly.

I try to answer his questions thoughtfully while enjoying the music and watching the activity in and around the courtyard, which is fascinating all on its own.

I am facing the entrance to the courtyard, which is full of people coming and going behind a line of people who are listening to the music. The musicians sit to my right at about two o'clock, and rows of people, three to four deep, attend them on either side. The area in front of the musicians remains open; while they perform, people walk forward and leave rupee bills in front of them on the ground, which are quickly picked up by a gentleman sitting with the musicians. There looks to be about eight of them, two playing harmonium, the rest with percussion instruments.

The temple sits directly in front of the musicians, and I become captivated by a young man—maybe nineteen or twenty—wearing a white cap and a gold brocade vest who is intent on keeping the crowd moving from one side of the courtyard to the next. As people pass, he motions with his hands for them to keep moving in whatever direction they're headed. The moment anyone stops to watch the music or take a picture, he does not hesitate to gently push or pull them beyond the area between the musicians and the temple. If he had a whistle and a uniform, he could be plunked in the middle of a busy urban intersection and look right at home.

I am curious about this young man. He seems to take his job very seriously. I don't think that's a bad thing—I always appreciate someone giving his or her all to the task at hand—but his sense of urgency seems out of proportion to the situation. Not that I know why he is doing what he's doing, but since it looks to be mere crowd control—keeping the flow of pedestrian traffic steady to avoid logjams—I find the energy he puts into his efforts remarkable. Later on, I learn it was his job to ensure the musicians maintained a clear line of sight to the temple in order to bring forth the most inspired vocals possible. Upon learning this, his energy makes perfect sense.

Watching all of this and conversing with my new chatty friend, I let my mind wander to the moment I sat here four years ago. At the end of that day, I was still in a state of disbelief that I was in India. As the music played, with the singers' improvisational lyrics and melodies rising up above the organ-like sound of the harmonium, I couldn't stop crying. *How is it possible for the world to hold so much beauty in so many faraway places?* I wondered. *What have I done to deserve such a rarified glimpse into the lives and faith of people on the other side of the planet?* I wanted to take the entire scene and trap it in glass, like a glimmering marble I could roll around in the palm of my hand. I wanted to be able to pull it out whenever I needed a reminder of how much magic the world is capable of creating every single day.

Tonight my attention is pulled in too many directions for the same kind of emotion to flow, but holding the memory steady in my mind in this moment is enough. My experience of listening to live music has looked like so many different things—the Go-Go's in eighth grade; Bruce Springsteen in tenth. I wept during the opera *La Bohème* and while singing with my whole heart at a packed church in San Francisco. Tears came to my eyes over a mojito in Havana the instant the sound of a violin wafted over our table, making me suddenly miss my husband—a violinist—terribly.

Of all the different forms of creative expression, music has the greatest power to pull emotion out of me as easily as a magician pulls a long string of silk scarves out of an apparently empty hand. Sitting here at the Hazrat Nizamuddin Dargah with my friends, surrounded by people of many nationalities and faiths—Muslims, Hindus, and Christians—I envision the music washing over all of us like water. All at once, we are clean, submerged in the stories being sung, sharing a communal experience that won't ever happen again. I might come back here one day, and maybe others here will too, but the universe we are creating together right now is singular. The precise arrangement of tonight's crowd will never exist again.

With this in mind, I close my eyes and let myself float. My spirit rises up and then looks down to survey the scene below. It makes up such a tiny part of the world, barely bigger than a high school gymnasium, but right now it is all I need to know. Whatever my questions and longings, they can be answered right here, in the music and the light and the love, in the mysterious wonder of it all.

The peacock became the
national bird of India
in 1963. Indigenous to
India, Nepal, Bangladesh,
Myanmar, and Sri Lanka,
it represents wisdom
in Buddhist philosophy.

This is India: throngs of people, dogs, cows, motorcycles, camels, buses, pigs, bicycles, rickshaws, elephants, mopeds, monkeys, horses, goats, and donkeys, all weaving and bobbing around one another in a mad ballet of forward motion. It is piles of trash the size of a minivan a stone's throw from carefully swept storefronts. It is boys crowded around a small, portable TV (one that looks exactly like the one I had in my bedroom in high school—in the eighties) with gold-and-glitter-festooned Bollywood dancers bouncing across the the screen. It is women carrying babies, men fixing motorcycles, and children playing cricket. It is the artfully arranged displays of fruit and vegetables on round metal tables with legs that teeter on uneven pavement. It is the rainbow of saris worn by women breaking up dirt and stones with pickaxes along the side of a rural road.

At every turn, India offers glimpses of the prosaic yet intimate routines of human beings everywhere—people walking, cycling, bathing, shaving, praying, cooking, driving, talking, buying, selling, urinating, sweeping, begging, eating, honking, napping, daydreaming, worshipping, and hauling firewood. A woman on the back of a motorcycle holds a baby goat. A toddler sits on the curb of a busy multi-lane thoroughfare watching traffic whiz by his tiny bare feet. I sit in one of the city's infamous traffic snarls, looking past the cars ahead of us, and notice a man going from car to car asking for money. This isn't a wildly shocking scene—until he walks out from behind a truck and I see he has no arms.

It is all this and so much more—sights, smells, sounds, and sensations coming at me with the speed and force of a tennis ball machine gone haywire. As I move through India's city streets, whether on foot or from the vantage point of a motorized rickshaw, everything passes so quickly, it is almost as if traces of every person, animal, and building are pulled out from behind them like wisps of cotton candy. My memories are constructed not with the static, unfixed appearance of objects at rest but with these faint trails of existence and purpose that become loosely knitted together over time.

This sensation is only amplified when my compatriots and I take a three-hour guided bicycle ride through Delhi. Starting at dawn, we are led through a maze of narrow alleyways and encouraged to make good (meaning constant) use of the clangy bike bell attached to our handlebars, a directive that helps us make sense of the unrelenting cacophony of India's congested roads. In America, I make use of my horn at times of distress and frustration. It is an auditory message board of sorts, where what I communicate is based on how firmly and how long I maintain pressure on the horn:

> *Excuse me, but the light has turned green!*
> *Watch out! I'm right here!*
> *MOVE IT, MORON!!!!*

In India, vehicle-related warning devices are utilized less for trying to express annoyance and more for ensuring everyone's presence is known:

> *I'm behind you!*
> *I'm next to you!*
> *Don't forget I'm behind you!*
> *Hey! I'm right here!*
> *I mean it! Don't forget I'm behind you!*

Whatever crosses our path—a person on foot, a cow, a dog, or someone on a scooter—it is our job, first and foremost, to alert everyone of our presence. While doing so, we must also be on the lookout for potholes, uneven pavement, trash, poop, and the occasional lone brick.

However fast life seemed to move when we walked through the textile and spice markets of Chandni Chowk yesterday, it is in full throttle today as I try to maneuver my way past Butcher's Alley (exactly what it sounds like), Turkman Gate, and the Red Fort. This is true until I become ensnared in an alleyway traffic jam, which finds me momentarily caught between a truck, a motorcycle, and a few stray dogs.

Riding a bicycle in Delhi requires a confident determination to keep moving coupled with a willingness to be patient while any vehicle, animal, or pedestrian blockage becomes untangled. (Although once said congestion clears up, I must *immediately* shift back to a focus on purposeful forward momentum or risk being, at best, a total annoyance or, at worst, run over.)

My memory of the same bicycle ride in 2014 is that it was a wild and crazy exploit. But as I try to stay in a single-file line today with our eight-person group as we wind through the hazards and distractions along our route, adrenaline pounds through my body like a tsunami. I wonder why this experience feels so different from the previous one. Why am I so much more nervous? Why does it feel so much more harrowing? It is exhilarating, yes, and also terrifying. While riding, I believe I am a badass superhero and also *insane*.

I think back to my experience in 2014. When we set out on two wheels that day, I started out reticent and slightly fearful but determined, and I finished feeling exuberant. This time my emotions from start to finish are flip-flopped; the first dauntless spins of my pedals give way to a rising panic that perhaps I've pushed my luck in signing up for this particular endeavor twice.

Maybe it is because there are now four of us to be concerned about instead of just two, or maybe it's that I'm more aware of all the possibilities that exist for something to go horribly wrong. It doesn't help that the tour company's other two customers in our group haven't been terribly interested in following the directives of our guides. They ride alongside me instead of in single file, which we were, with good reason, explicitly instructed to do.

I am the last person to arrive at the place where we will have an early lunch. I am wound up, slightly shaken, and wildly irritated at the two other riders for not only dismissing our guide's instructions but also weaving in and out of the line Jennette, Barb, Kolleen, and I were eager to keep intact, which caused us to lose sight of each other every so often. When I wound up at the end of the line behind one of these riders, whose sluggish turn into the last alleyway caused me to slow down, feel the bike wobble, lose my balance, and fall into the wall, my frustration became hard to contain.

Once I arrive at the meeting place for lunch and get my bike situated amongst all the other parked bicycles, Barb grabs me, hugs me, and doesn't let go. She sees the way I'm crumpling and doesn't hesitate to swoop in and hold me up.

We walk into the restaurant, and our guide directs us to a large table, but Jennette steps forward and declares the four us are going to eat at our own table. I sit down at the table she's chosen feeling slightly defeated but in awe of my friends' support. I don't like that today's bike ride felt more daunting than it did four years ago, but they are showing up for me in this moment of vulnerability like warriors. There is no pity, no shame, no *Poor Christine*. They are gathering around and lifting me back up, letting me know I have nothing to be afraid of.

How many times have I felt compelled to put on a brave face in moments of discomfort, frustration, or even physical pain? What is it that has me thinking it is a good idea to steel myself against any outward signs of emotion in front of my friends? After spending much of my life believing it was better to buck up and keep a low profile, I am learning the futility of trying to construct a wall around myself in moments of anxiety, fear, and desperation.

In India, this is even more pronounced, for the simple reason that

I would rather direct my energies toward enjoying my time here than toward trying to prevent my friends from knowing how much I'm struggling in this moment. Lucky for me, they know me well enough that I have no hope of hiding something like this. It creates a moment of intimacy that ends up being one of the sweetest experiences of this trip. This morning's bike ride knocked me off kilter in more ways than I was expecting, but I am reminded of something I won't soon forget: I will always be taken care of; I am deeply loved.

We finish our meal and get ourselves ready for the last leg of our ride, and I know the best thing I can do is simply take it all in—to let my heart pound, to feel my lungs pump, to let myself be invigorated in a way that might not ever happen again. One thing is impossible to deny on this morning, which is that *I am alive.*

By the end of our morning adventure, the day is in full swing. The Day-Glo orange disk that hovered in the sky at eye level when we started is now above us, the misty gray haze giving way to a faint veil of clouds that lets the blue skies beyond it seep through like a mirage. Traffic zips along, blaring its wild chorus of horns, bells, and beeps like a stampede of motorized cattle.

As we return our matching orange bicycles, I conjure up an image of my husband back home—he would be fast asleep there now—and marvel at the simultaneity of life around the world. Morning in Delhi is, all at once, nighttime in Milwaukee, mid-afternoon in Tokyo, and just before dawn in Reykjavik. Whatever we are doing—me and all my fellow humans—each of us carries an entire universe with us wherever we go. As we move through our days, one after another, our individual solar systems contract, expand, and evolve, all while passing through and crashing into each other and thus writing the story of our world. Even a monk on a mountaintop in Nepal is part of the global dance.

As I envision myself as one small part of this immense whole, my very physicality feels impalpable, as if I'm not quite solid and therefore not as separate from others as I sometimes think I am. This might not be my country, but it is my world, our world. We are all, whether we care to admit it or not, in this wild ride together. Wherever all these people and creatures are going, whatever it is they are trying to do or see, they are, just like me, giving birth to an expansive universe of experiences and memories, moment by moment by moment. As soon as our paths cross, their story becomes my story, and vice versa. We are all trying to make our way through a big, wide world while at the mercy of life's whims and twists of fate. We are all still becoming. We are all made of stars.

Sunrise on the Yamuna

After being instructed to remove our shoes and socks and to cover our heads with scarves, I take my first step beyond the enclosed, carpeted space that marks our entrance to the temple grounds of the Gurudwara Bangla Sahib—and that's when the memory comes flooding back to me. The tiled marble walkway, which has a milky texture of creams and whites, is *cold*—cold in a way that feels vibrant and precious, as if I am walking on a giant slab of pearl just extracted from the depths of the ocean. I had forgotten this sensation from my visit four years ago and now become fixated on it, determined never to let this particular detail escape me again. When I look up and see the last stretch before the entrance to the central shrine is covered by a long carpet, I feel slightly deflated. I like the way the cold, which is a hair's breadth from uncomfortable, has me feeling the bottoms of my feet.

Within the temple, it is the *kirtan*—Sikhism's devotional singing—that holds me rapt. What I hear is known as a *raga*, a melodic framework for improvisation, with recitations of Sikh scriptures and legends comprising the lyrics. The performance is a mystical blend of voice, harmonium, and *tabla*, or drum. The musicians are situated beneath an arched, canopied platform made entirely of gold, which is itself enveloped in a space covered with gold bas relief from the floor to thirty-foot ceiling and more scalloped archways. A three-tiered, circular, crystal chandelier hangs above it all, amplifying and refracting the gilt, creating an aurelian scene that manages to feel both futuristic and ancient, as if I am walking into a life-sized diorama of what future earthlings might imagine of their fifteenth-century ancestors. A constant, whispering stream of people, very few of whom are Westerners, moves through the shrine.

Once I sit cross-legged on the carpeted floor, I become part of the congregation, or *sangat*, which, in ancient Indian text, is defined as "like-minded individuals, or fellow travelers, on a spiritual journey." It feels sacred, but in an exotic way, in a way that is clearly not my faith. Guru Nanak, the founder of Sikhism, is not my teacher, and these songs are not my hymns, but I am moved to tears nonetheless. As the sounds of mournful chants curl around me like silk ribbons, I let my body sink into the moment.

Our time in India has barely begun, and already I feel my cells rearranging themselves. I am a different person from who I was the day we landed, different from when I first set foot in this temple not ten minutes earlier. Every moment, some part of me is changing, a process that contracts and expands in direct proportion to my willingness to release my judgments, expectations, and assumptions. I can't stop myself from having thoughts about what I see and experience; the trick is not to believe them. Listening to the *kirtan*, I know there is nothing I need to believe or disbelieve. There is only this moment and all the beauty around me.

I don't want to leave the music and the gold and the stillness, but we are excited to visit the kitchen and become part of a team preparing lunch for ten thousand guests. It is a daily offering here at Gurudwara Bangla Sahib: a substantive vegetarian lunch for whomever walks in their door. Believed to have been started by Guru Nanak, the langar was intended as an expression of "equality between all people regardless of religion, caste, colour, creed, age, gender or social status." While partaking in a menu consisting of rice, *dahl* (cooked lentils), cumin-spiced potatoes, and other accompaniments, guests sit on narrow mats on the floor, side by side and back to back, with covered heads and bare feet.

The *langar* is served in a separate building, away from the shrine, and the lunch service has not yet begun. The dining hall floors are still being mopped while a small group of people in an alcove outside the main entrance chops onions. Although there will soon be somewhere in the vicinity of ten thousand hungry souls to feed, the kitchen is surprisingly serene, equipped with oversized cookware and utensils befitting such an enterprise. There are thirty-pound bags of salt piled ten high, copper pots big enough for me to sit inside, and ladles the size of a grapefruit. No one rushes anywhere, and all movements—stirring, rolling out dough, and flipping *roti* (a flat, round bread) on a grill—are delicate and precise.

After walking the full perimeter of the primary kitchen, which is about half the size of a football field, we end up seated on a long, narrow bench a few inches above the ground in front of a slab of marble covered in flour. When Jennette and I sit down next to each other, no one explains what our job is; we're simply handed a small, well-worn rolling pin and a few balls of dough. I become immediately, wholeheartedly immersed in the task at hand, dropping into the moment like a stone in water—dough, flour, roll, stack, again and again and again.

During the brief instances I look up to see what's happening around me, I notice everyone in pairs, starting with a chatty gentleman in a black turban giving instructions to Kolleen to my left. Across the way, an Indian woman in her early thirties wearing jeans and a striped sweater is deep in conversation with Barb, and I can't help but notice Barb's red plaid vest is almost an exact match of the red plaid scarf on the woman's head. Two older Indian women in saris on the far end of the marble work area sit to my right, and I relish the way they give Jennette and I subtle nods of encouragement as they toss balls of dough for us to roll into thin pancakes about the size of our hand.

No one is telling me what I'm doing wrong or how I could be doing my job better. When someone comes over to pick up my stack of twenty or so *rotis*, they make no comment on my technique. There is no sense that anything has to be perfect or even that what we are doing is terribly remarkable, as if feeding ten thousand people every day in the middle of

The main temple

Delhi is no big deal. But I think for everyone here, that is exactly the point. It isn't a big deal in the sense that anyone is looking for (or offering) credit or praise. This work is being done because it needs to be done, because hunger is hunger, whether it has been lingering since lunch the day before or has barely woken from its post-breakfast slumber. The *langar* is not about recognition but about being of service to whomever shows up in need of a hot meal.

I could say the same thing about my own home, which has been, wherever we've lived, a place of refuge for the people we love. Like the *langar*, my home has a certain order and beauty, which is supported by an intention of invitation. Whoever walks into our home needs to be made to feel welcome, comfortable, and peaceful. I do this with fresh flowers, small gifts in guest bedrooms, and fresh bars of soap in the shower. My husband does it in the kitchen, preparing and serving meals that are always preferable to a night of dining out.

We don't do this for accolades. We do not expect applause. There was no trophy awarded to us when we opened our home to my stepson and his wife for almost a year while they built their house or when we did the same thing for two of our best friends when they were out of work for five months. I don't iron our table linens hoping anyone will notice. My husband doesn't spend hours shopping for the best ingredients for a new recipe because he wants a medal.

We give our time and energy to these efforts out of love. We go to great lengths to create a cozy nest because it feels like the most natural thing in the world to do. The world can be a hard place, a place of struggle. If there's a way we can soften those edges for our loved ones, we will do it. This is our way of expressing love and being of service. Just like this place, my home is a temple. Within its walls, I can quietly make the world a better place.

When it comes time for us to depart, we simply get up and leave. Our time in the kitchen was barely an hour, and to everyone around us that is enough. While it is obvious the temple staff has a well-honed structure for getting the work done each day, it is also clear this system leaves plenty of room for the ebb and flow of irregular and transitory volunteers like us, which I come to see as the real magic of the *langar*. Everyone is welcome—to roll out dough, mop the floor, serve, eat, or clean up—and whatever role one plays, it is a necessary and meaningful contribution to the ensemble. We are all here for the same reason: to give, to receive, and to do it all with love.

Mother Teresa urges us to do small things with great love, which is precisely where I see the point of contact between God and India. It is why I tell people I've felt His presence here more than anywhere else, despite all of its troubling elements. How else can kindness, generosity, compassion, and humility be expressed *but* in the small things in a place like India?

What else explains the force behind the Bangla Sahib's free kitchen and its ability to so masterfully attend to the needs of its 3.65 million annual guests?

After returning to our hotel, as I organize my belongings for the next day's journey to Varanasi, I think back to my afternoon at the *langar*. When I imagine the trail of devotion that moved from the first scoop of flour to the rolling pin in my hands to the warm, crisp *roti* that was served to today's guests, I see the part I played in that flow. While there, I was able to sit down and roll out some dough, so that is what I did. It was small, but it was done with great love, just as Mother Teresa instructed.

Making roti for the Langar

ANNAPURNA

Annapurna Devi Mata is the Hindu goddess of food and nourishment, depicted with a vessel full of porridge and a golden ladle adorned with jewels. She is an avatar of Parvati, the wife of Shiva.

The city of Varanasi, also known as Benaras, sits on the west side of the Ganges. There are more than 1.2 million inhabitants of Varanasi, which covers an area of just over 32 square miles. My former home of Santa Barbara is slightly larger at about 42 square miles with only 92,000 residents. There are an estimated 23,000 temples, 84 ghats, and 15 mosques. The dominant industry is silk weaving, followed by tourism. It is believed that Buddha's first sermon — "The Setting in Motion of the Wheel of Dharma" — was made in nearby Sarnath around 528 B.C. It is the holiest of the seven sacred cities in India and an important place of pilgrimage for both Hindus and Buddhists.

JANUARY 13, 2018 *Varanasi Arrival*

My travel mates and I were told to prepare ourselves for Varanasi—that it isn't a place for the faint of heart, that life and death exist alongside each other here. These warnings weren't laced with panic; no one handed us a laundry list of dangers (aside from stories of mischievous monkeys grabbing purses and bags). They were offered as gentle nudges to prepare ourselves mentally and emotionally for this place that is neither subtle nor meek. Those who heard of our plans to visit Varanasi usually responded with a knowing "Aaaahhh," as if the mere thought of this city needed a tiny bit of space to settle in.

After arriving by plane from Delhi, our journey to the Ganges begins on a newly constructed multi-lane highway, which eventually leads to increasingly congested streets populated by the same kinds of crowds and activity we'd seen elsewhere: women in prismatic saris carrying bundles of wood on their heads, boys zipping through traffic on mopeds, and cows ambling past vegetable carts like they had all the time in the world (which I suppose they do in a country where nearly half the population is vegetarian). While we lumber down the road, I assume we will be dropped off at our hotel. We are instead deposited at the northern end of Varanasi, near the Rajghat bridge and the Ravidas Mandir temple. From there we are told we will be picked up and taken to our hotel by boat, about a ten-minute ride.

As we near the drop-off point, within sight of the water, we pass a tour bus filled not with white-skinned tourists but with Indians who, our tour guide explains, are in Varanasi for the Makar Sankranti festival. Occurring every January, it marks the first day of the transit of the sun—Surya—moving northward into winter solstice. One form of tribute to the sun involves flying kites, which we soon see twirling and swooping from rooftops all along the Ganges. Other forms of tribute include fireworks and ritual bathing at sunrise.

While we wait for our ride to the hotel, I become entranced by the activities of a baby goat that is wandering around the top of the steps. Wearing a tattered plaid wrap, he seems to belong to someone, although it isn't at all clear who, given the clusters of people in the vicinity. He moves as if held by an invisible tether to a larger goat, presumably his mama, gleefully bounding up and down the steps only to quickly return to her side. There is a world he is eager to explore, but it's an instinct he isn't quite ready to follow, as demonstrated by his propensity to suddenly and intermittently confirm she is always just a few steps away.

A few minutes later, as we drift lazily along the Ganges amidst a few dozen other boaters, we pass one *ghat*—a set of steps leading down to a river—after another, each marked by hand-painted signs on the buildings. There are bright yellow buildings, tangerine buildings, and buildings the same shade of turquoise as the waters of Kauai. And there are steps, endless steps, some sparsely occupied, others crowded, and still others covered by rows of freshly washed laundry drying in the sun—bold swatches of fabric the color of gumballs. There is color and activity everywhere as we pass *ghats* with names like Nishad, Telianala, Nandu, and Sheetla. There is Panchganga, Ganga Mahal, and Sankatha.

When we arrive at our destination and I walk up the steps from the Ganges, I notice a man sitting outside our hotel. A single piece of orange cloth is wrapped around his waist and then flung over one shoulder, and he wears multiple strands of wooden beads around his neck. He is covered in ash, and a long, dark beard and dreadlocks hang past his shoulders. He sits cross-legged in front of a makeshift fireplace, two large logs arranged within a tidy, two-layered row of weathered bricks, the flame barely visible from my vantage point. A gold trident with a copper sun at its center leans next to him against the wall. He is very still, unperturbed by anything going on around him. He is thin but not skeletal, maybe forty-five years old, although if you tell me he is ten years younger or older, I would believe you.

Another twenty feet or so beyond him sits another holy man, this one with a shaved head, his body covered in a white garment and a deep aqua blue shawl. He, too, is seated cross-legged on what looks like a yoga mat that is the color of a perfect blue sky. His head is bowed in the same way as my favorite wooden Buddha statue back home.

We landed in Varanasi less than two hours ago, and already I feel like I've been transported into another realm.

Marigolds at the Ganges

JANUARY 13, 2018 *Ganga Aarti*

The Ganga Aarti holds nothing back in the way of theatrics and choreography. On this, our first evening in Varanasi, we are kept enthralled by the sensory explosion of this ceremony, which is held every evening in Varanasi at the Dasaswamedh *ghat*, just a short walk from our hotel.

After opening the ceremony with the blowing of a conch shell, seven Brahmin priests perform a precise series of motions on elevated platforms, all in homage to "Mama Ganga"—the Ganges River. The ceremony is all light and smoke and clanging bells. The priests send up offerings of sandalwood powder, camphor, ghee, and incense in all four directions, and they throw marigolds in the air at various intervals. Beyond the bright lights above the platforms, the river is dotted with candlelight from the *diyas* (tea light candles surrounded by flowers in shallow paper or tin bowls) that have been released into the water by worshippers.

Visitors watch the ceremony from rows of plastic chairs, from the surrounding balconies (where we are), and from boats tightly packed together in the river, most of which are wooden, long, and varied in color. The majority of people in the boats are Indian, their faces vibrant and eager. While the bright lights shine on their faces, the darkness, tinged with a golden-gray haze cast by the delicate evening fog, fades into the background.

While considered by some to be too theatrical for genuine spiritual inspiration, I am astonished that this production happens every day. I promise myself I will remember the ceremony when I am back home, that I will envision it in the mornings when I drink my coffee, which is when the Ganga Aarti will be happening here, not only in Varanasi, but also in Haridwar and Rishikesh. I savor the knowledge that as I fry eggs and butter toast back home, seven Hindu priests will be paying homage to their holy river, their acts shining light on the faces of all the pilgrims, whether seated, standing, or bobbing on the water.

Devotion is Varanasi's calling card; it is the thing that drives most of the actions and expressions I see around me here. The Aarti ceremony punctuates the evening with a dazzling exclamation point, which is fitting for a day that was filled with lessons in various devotions. For worshippers who have come to Varanasi to fulfill a lifelong dream of cleansing away their sins in the Ganges, the spectacle makes sense. These rites and rituals deserve such a celebration, one filled with light, sound, and music spectacular enough to reach the heavens.

The Ganga Aarti in full swing

It is morning, and we're up early for our first full day in Varanasi. Breakfast feels like a decadent affair, with our being offered as much masala chai as we want while I imagine the local *sadhu* I'd spotted yesterday continuing his sedentary vigil outside. The city was wrapped in a blanket of silvery fog when I stepped onto the hotel's balcony before breakfast, the scene creating a lyrical, auditory dreamscape as all the sounds below me wafted up, layer upon layer: the muffled din of voices and the higher-pitched squeals of children, both nearly consumed by a circular, almost monotone chorus that wasn't quite a chant and wasn't quite a song but evoked images of men in orange robes laying tiny bowls of marigolds in the Ganges.

My inability to locate the physical origin of each sound and see where they were coming from, to see *anything*, provided an unexpected sense of relief—a respite from all the moments I've had so far where my senses were overloaded by stimuli assaulting me from all directions. It has been a tricky dilemma, wanting desperately not to miss anything but knowing the futility of trying to capture it all. Those few moments on our hotel's balcony showed me exactly what the nature of my memories will be when I get back home: incomplete, foggy, and full of things I can't see but I know are there nonetheless, just beyond my grasp.

"Doubt is in the mind. And faith is in the heart." So proclaims our Varanasi tour guide, Dinesh, as he launches into his description of what we will see today, an explanation that isn't merely about what temples and shrines we will visit but about why Varanasi is considered the holiest of the seven sacred cities in India. Jennette, Kolleen, Barb, and I are enthralled, grateful for a guide who seems to instinctively know what we are looking for in Varanasi: God.

We never explicitly said this to each other, that we want to find God in India, but it is in our nature, all of us, to be constantly seeking what is sacred, holy, and ineffable. We never needed to state outright that our deepest longing for India had to do with the expansion of our faith or the evolution of our soul. We know this about each other as well as we know the contours of one another's faces. Over the course of many years, we have consciously, intentionally built our friendships on a foundation of spiritual curiosity, soulful creativity, and divine feminine wisdom. Whether creating ceremonies for each other, leading women's circles, or providing a safe space for the expression of our messier human moments, our most fundamental encouragement of each other usually ends up pointing in the same direction: to God, and to prayer.

We have also each come to India on the other side of a major life passage. I have just moved across country, Jennette is recently divorced, and Kolleen is in the first stage of a major career shift. While here, Barb will honor the one-year anniversary of the death of her mom. Within each of us, a delicate, vulnerable being is in the process of taking her first wobbly steps into a brave new world within. India doesn't offer precise instructions for how to fortify the strength we need to move confidently forward; its magic is in the way it shows us how to see the world and our place in it—that whatever has happened before and whatever might take place later, we serve ourselves, and God, best by surrendering to the flow of *what is*. In India, this is our most important practice.

By the time we set out for the day's adventures, all that was murky and hidden earlier in the morning has come alive in full color. We make our way toward a nearby *ghat*, which has us navigating slippery, uneven steps through crowds of holy men, souvenir hawkers, and morning bathers, many of whom are here on pilgrimage for the Makar Sankranti festival. The mood is buoyant and lively, even as many people stop mid-motion at the sight of our merry band of four.

Looking down, where the steps disappear into the Ganges, bathers take their own approach to communion with the river. It is, for the most part, delineated across gender lines. Most of the men opt for repeated, full, underwater submersion—dunking, floating, and swimming—while women cluster in small groups in knee-high water, splashing it on their faces and bodies repeatedly, their fully soaked saris clinging to their skin. Everyone is in various states of undress, but no one is naked. Many collect water in large plastic jugs. Laughter and lightheartedness float in the midst of a monumentally sacred experience, the fulfillment of a lifelong dream for some.

Vendors try to sell us postcards, lotus bead necklaces, and blessings, the latter of which I accept, paying ten rupees for a dab of sandalwood powder on my forehead and a prayer said in my honor. We pass groups of women walking together in single file, most of whom extend a blank stare that melts into delighted acknowledgment once one of us offers a head bobble or smile. All four of us are smitten by pretty much everyone. While most exchanges involve nothing beyond "Namaste" and a selfie or two, our mutual affection gushes like a fire hydrant sprung open. We fall immediately in love with each other and then, just as quickly, must say goodbye.

My attention darts in different directions like a pinball machine in an effort to manage a laundry list of pursuits. I want to take in all the sights around me, exchange smiles with the locals, and listen to everything Dinesh is saying. At the same time, I need to be careful not to lose sight of my friends, step in animal poop, or twist an ankle on the uneven pavement. I have to be mindful of the stray kite strings that keep getting tangled in my feet, and I need to allow plenty of room for all the cows, dogs, and goats that cross my path. It doesn't feel stressful, but it is an exercise in extreme multitasking, where my journey from Point A to Point B does not allow for untethered daydreaming or distraction. With every step I take, I must account for and process as much as possible in order to avoid any number of discomfiting mishaps.

It is part of the wild ride of being a tourist in India, this acute attention to detail, and might very well be at the heart of why India inspires responses that fall at either end of the spectrum. If I didn't feel exhilarated by all the ways India pushes me out of my comfort zone, I would not gently drift toward incertitude; I would likely want to leave as soon as humanly possible and never return. Visitors to India rarely say their experience was "pretty good" or "somewhat interesting"; they either fall madly in love with the country or adopt an acronym that made perfect sense to me when I heard it: I'm Never Doing India Again.

It isn't so much that I thrive on discomfort but that the particular challenges of India bring into sharp focus my ability to choose how I am going to respond to everything. Am I going to get upset, shut down, act out? Or might it be better to accept something unexpected, let it go, and use my energy to enjoy the rest of the day? Whatever situation I find myself in, I always know one thing for certain: in every moment, I have the power to choose how I respond, what to focus on, and whether or not to hold on to it once it has passed.

India isn't merely a place I like to explore but an invitation to spend time with my deepest philosophies about myself, my life, and the world. What do I believe, and why do I believe it? Which beliefs contribute to the quality of my life, and which ones diminish it? Those questions can be answered in the way I move through India, in the way I respond to everything India decides to throw at me. Do I believe I am safe? Do I believe I need to be in control? What are my expectations, and how will I respond if they are not met? What do I believe about my friends, especially in the moments when all of our quirks and fears and longings collide?

I can be the kind of person I want to be when I'm sunk deep in my favorite chair at home, Tilda at my feet, a cup of tea by my side. What kind of person do I want to be—what kind of person am I capable of being—when it's three in the afternoon and I haven't eaten since breakfast, my home is 7,500 miles away, and I have to pee so bad my eyeballs hurt? During these fourteen days I am in India, I know I will find out, and I know it is those lessons and revelations that will end up being the most meaningful treasures I take home.

Entrance to a private home

LORD SHIVA

Legend says Varanasi was founded by
the god Shiva, one of the principal deities
of Hinduism. As the supreme being who
creates, protects, and transforms the universe,
Shiva is depicted with a serpent around
his neck, the crescent moon, and the holy
river Ganges flowing from his hair.

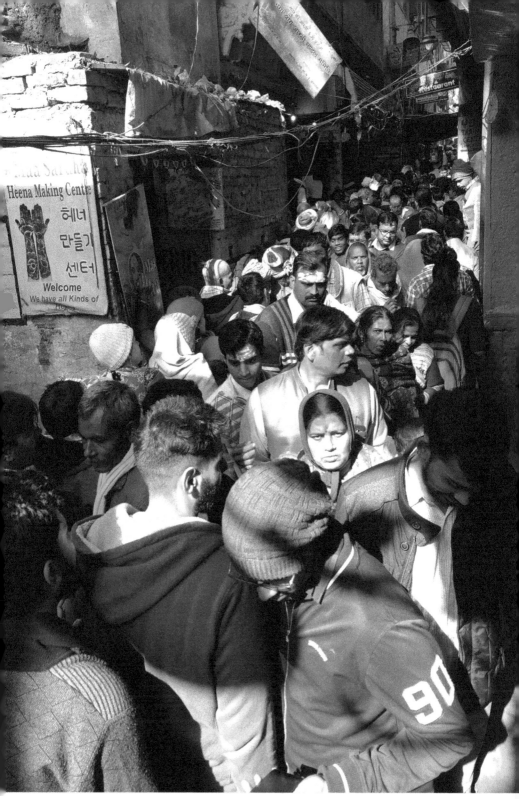

JANUARY 14, 2018 *The Golden Temple*

Dinesh tells us we are going to the Golden Temple, named so for the gleaming, gold-plated domes and spires that sit atop the main structure. Formally known as the Shri Kashi Vishwanath Temple, it is tucked within the maze of small lanes just beyond sight of the Ganges. Considering the swarms of people we left behind in the wide-open expanse of the steps, it is surprisingly quiet as we follow a path that is all angles and curves and so narrow we need to walk single file most of the time. We pass a turquoise blue structure adorned with a painting of Lakshmi, a shrine dedicated to Durga, and a tangled tree trunk growing out of the building it is attached to.

Suddenly, and seemingly out of nowhere, the population swells, and we are corralled into a narrow corridor that splits men apart from women and where we have to show our passports and the contents of our bags to uniformed guards. This does not lead us into the temple but another narrow lane—the longest one we've seen so far—with a thick line of people. To my left, the rolling metal door of a small shop is closed, but the vendor just beyond it is open, its proprietor reading the paper. Dinesh has a quick word with him, and before we have time to ask him what was said, the sliding door is pulled open and we are invited to sit down inside.

The view is a sea of humanity. It is middle-aged men, elderly matriarchs, and young women in their twenties, many of whose foreheads are marked with sandalwood powder and turmeric. They are wearing striped collared shirts, plaid shawls, ribbed wool caps, and turbans the color of mustard. Carrying baskets of fruit, incense, and flowers, they form a shapeless mass that contracts and expands to make room for whoever needs to pass through, be it a person or a cow.

The four of us have gone as far as we will be allowed to go. A normal day at the Kashi Vishwanath boasts an average of three thousand visitors, but today we are in the midst of a festival, so the crowds are especially heavy. The concern that one of us might get lost in the throngs is not an overly cautious one. Dinesh's determination to keep us somewhat sequestered in our tiny viewing area is prudent, and none of us is disappointed to be relieved of the burden of trying not to lose each other. If anything, we relish the opportunity to sit quietly and soak it all in, to be nothing more than part of the scenery for all the people in front of us who have traveled from who knows how far away to be blessed at this temple and its river.

The temple is another part of Varanasi where life and death meld. It is not a cremation area, but visitors come here with the fate of their soul and spirit on their mind, as the Kashi Vishwanath is one of the most famous Hindu temples dedicated to Lord Shiva. Through devotion to Shiva, pilgrims are offered a trifecta of stamps in their spiritual passport. A bath in the Ganges, a visit to the Kashi Vishwanath temple, and, upon death, cremation are all rituals and places of worship for Hindu pilgrims on their quest for *moksha*—liberation from *samsara*, the cycle of rebirth. While some pilgrims arrive in Varanasi with the bodies of their loved ones to assist them on this path, everyone in front of us is here in pursuit of their own salvation.

While silently observing, I notice three women talking together. One of them catches my eye, and it doesn't take long before I realize why: she reminds me of my grandma. Wearing a bright green sari with gold trim, she is tall and slender, built exactly like my grandma. Once I fixate on her, I can't stop staring, until I turn around to Dinesh and ask him to call her over to us. She obliges, and I hold out my hand to her as she approaches.

"Can you please tell her she reminds me of my grandma?" I ask Dinesh as the woman and I join hands.

He says this to her in Hindi, and she and I exchange wide smiles. I look as deeply into her eyes as I can in the midst of the crowds, the language barrier, and the very limited amount of time we have with each other, wanting to simultaneously give and receive. I want her to know how much this brief exchange means to me, and I want to see if there is anything else in her—something deep, something within her soul—that will also give me a glimpse of my grandma, who passed away just over twelve years ago.

The connection I shared with my grandma was like a thick, braided rope spun of gold. Our relationship began with my summer visits to Oklahoma, where she lived, when I was a kid and extended all the way to the period when she moved from the home she'd lived in for most of her adult life to a nursing home. In between, she offered support, encouragement, and guidance as I made my way through college, graduate school, my first marriage, starting my own business, my divorce, and what was, at the time of her transition to the nursing home, a new relationship with the man who would become my second husband.

When the woman returns to her friends, I keep watching her—and then I see it. It lasts less than a full second—a flash of an instant, come and gone in a blink—but it is there, and I believe it with everything I am. I have goosebumps and immediately start crying. It is my grandma's smile and, I am certain, my grandma.

By the time she died, my grandma was eighty-six and had lived a good life. While I was heartbroken to lose her, I wasn't devastated. If anything, I was relieved for her, excited for her to be finally free to travel wherever she wanted. It was how I saw her the day she passed away and how I have continued to see her every day since—as a bird, the wind, the trees, the very air I breathe. While I've missed her physical presence—the feel of her hand in mine, the sound of her voice over the phone—once she was gone, I have seen and felt her *everywhere*. Through the release of her physical self, her spirit could soar and expand throughout the entire universe. *She* was an entire universe.

No matter what goal or dream I pursued, my grandma had a way of nudging me forward, letting me know she was right beside me, cheering me on every step of the way. Sometimes she did this with a letter, other times a phone call. On many occasions it involved thick packets in the mail, full of articles and clippings she thought I'd find interesting.

Seeing my grandma appear in the smile of a woman I happened to cross paths with outside a Hindu temple in Varanasi doesn't feel outrageous or wishful. It feels magical and soulful and perfect, like it is the most obvious thing in the world. Here I am, in the midst of another personal exploration, and then . . . there she is, making me realize how much I have been longing for a sign that I am on the right path, that she is proud of me still.

Before too long, all four of us are in need of a tissue.

"Now it is coming," declares Dinesh, his acknowledgment of the emotion Varanasi is capable of inspiring. "Some people listen to me talk with arms crossed and face blank, and they are here to check items off of a list. But if you can open your heart and let the emotions come in, you can feel God."

He is not at all surprised by our outpouring; he is enlivened by it. In him we have found a kindred spirit, the person we believe was meant to be our guide during our few days in this city.

I came here wanting to find God, hopeful I'd feel His presence. If I'd had any doubt He was here waiting for me, it just evaporated like steam from a teakettle. While sitting with my friends as the woman turned and walked away, I heard Him, loud and clear: "Hey, there. Got your message. I know you've been looking for Me, so I thought I'd drop in and let you know: I'm here—with your grandma—and we love you."

As we wrap up our morning at the temple and make our way back to the river, I am giddy and humbled. I never asked my grandma to meet me in India. It never occurred to me I might see her. But there she was, plain as day, clothed in dark skin and gold jewelry, smiling her magnificent smile.

A sadhu is a religious ascetic, mendicant (monk), or any holy person in Hinduism and Jainism who has renounced the worldly life.

JANUARY 15, 2018 *Moksha*

Varanasi hugs the Ganges in the shape of a boomerang. The northeast end of it, where we boarded our boat the day we arrived, is the top of the boomerang. About a quarter of the way down, along the top of the curve, is the Manikarnika *ghat*, which can be seen from a distance every time we've approached it. We don't see the *ghat*, actually, but the smoke, which is how the Manikarnika can be identified. After all the color, texture, and vibrancy of the views we've taken in so far, we glide toward the source of the steady plumes of dark smoke, where the buildings are tinted sepia and charcoal, stains created by the constant output of soot and ash.

It is here where the photos I've seen countless times on travel websites and in guidebooks for India come to life in all their dark and somber reality. As we pass, we see what is, for this precise part of the world, normal: twenty-four hours a day, seven days a week, Hindu mourners bring the bodies of their loved ones for a ritual burning at the Ganges, believing the deceased will attain *moksha*, or liberation from the cycle of rebirth. Up to three hundred bodies are burned each day in Varanasi, aided by *doms*—members of a caste of "untouchables" who are paid by individual families to assist in the cremation, some of whose families have been doing this work for seven generations.

We are taken to the cremation area by boat on numerous occasions during our time in Varanasi, and each time I keep thinking I will feel more . . . *something*. I'm not sure if I was expecting to be more horrified or that, when confronted with death so viscerally, I would be granted some new sense of presence or gratitude or awe at simply being alive. What I feel more than anything is a fascination about all that is happening around the burning bodies. There is a reason and a purpose for everything, and there is a story about everything, and I am struck by the carefully scripted rites and rituals.

It is smoky, sooty, and crowded on this particular *ghat*, and the burning area isn't organized to provide privacy or clear lines of delineation. No one shows up with the body of their loved one and is told to carry it to Row A, Platform 12. But even so, none of the moving parts is random; each one is part of the same shadowy, poetic dance. Even the cows I see hanging around the periphery of the cremation area are there for a reason: to gobble up leftover marigolds that, just hours before, adorned the bodies.

More than anything, I am moved by the faith all these mourners hold in their hearts. That they are willing to carry the body of someone they loved dearly down narrow, crowded streets, sometimes at night, sometimes in broad daylight. That they make the effort to adorn the shrouded figure with red and gold fabric, fresh flowers, oils, and herbs. That they take the body down to the Ganges as a final preparation for cremation. That they purchase 300 kilograms (more than 600 pounds) of wood, arrange it in a certain way, cover the body with ghee and sandalwood powder, and ignite the pyre themselves. That they stay with the body while it burns, a three- to four-hour endeavor. Women are not permitted to be part of these rituals, as their sadness and tears are believed to be too great, which would threaten to keep the soul of the deceased attached to this life.

At the end of all this, the soul is liberated. From Varanasi, it goes to meet God.

The day we arrived I saw only a few bodies burning; this evening, I count thirteen. No matter what time of day or what day of the week, the cremation process is an act of love that is anything but comfortable, sterile, or tidy. There is no hiding from the fact that this is death and that there will come a time when I, too, will pass from this world—and that the world will keep going on without me, as evidenced by the people washing laundry just a few *ghats* away.

In Varanasi, life goes on not just beyond death but in the midst of it. Life and death are not mere neighbors, separated by fences and walls and windows, but spiritual spouses, curling around each other like two snails in a single shell. They are not separate experiences that constitute a beginning and an ending but rather, together, provide the most fundamental and basic foundation that enables the flow—and expansion—of our existence.

The Manikarnika ghat

The sight of burning bodies does not disturb me. It is peaceful and inspires a deep internal silence. I am not witnessing an experience peculiar to India. I am getting a glimpse of my own impermanence, of the ultimate physical transformation of every living creature on earth. I believe I am more than just my physical self, and this is a belief I share with everyone who has brought the body of their loved one to this place.

Even if my version of life beyond our earthly existence looks different from everyone around me, we agree there is more to us than just the raw material of our bodies, and I find that a source of great comfort and connection. I recognize it isn't my body that contains my soul but my soul that provides the home for my body—a home for all the ways my physical self can express what I know to be bigger than me and beyond my full comprehension, things like love and faith and goodness.

Because what is it, really, that compels me to want to live by a certain code—to be kind, to live honestly, to be a force for good in the world in whatever way I am able? Are these values inspired by and in service to my physical self or my soul? Or is it something else entirely—namely, God? And if it turns out I am being guided by my faith—by my relationship with God—more than any other title I could claim in this world (wife, artist, daughter, writer), then I have no reason to be fearful of the day I am called to shed my physical self and pass on from this world.

Tonight, our last evening in Varanasi, while observing a ritual that is thousands of years old, I gaze at my friends and the man steering our boat. I contemplate the mourners, the cows, the dogs, the other boaters, and the kids flying kites from the tops of buildings. I think of my husband; of our dog, Tilda; of my mom and my dad. I don't move a muscle as our boat gently bobs in the water. I watch the flames stretch upward, toward heaven. The sky above is dark, but everyone's face is aglow. Flowers are placed all around us. A paper lantern floats in the sky. I am empty, and formless, and filled with light. For an instant, it feels entirely possible to swallow the moon.

JANUARY 16, 2018 *More*

It is our last day in Varanasi, and we are preparing for the next leg of our journey. According to our plans, we will return to Varanasi's airport, fly to Delhi, fly to Jaipur, and then take a ninety-minute drive north to Samode Village.

The tickle I felt in my throat in Delhi has now morphed into a full-blown cough and cold, and Jennette is also struggling with a cough, cold, and severe body aches. It is a familiar feeling, being sick in India, since Barb and I dealt with the same issues four years ago, and I am responding now the way I did then. Grateful my illness has nothing to do with anything gastrointestinal, my approach is to make good use of the arsenal of cold medications I brought with me and to surge ahead. I feel like crap, but it is a manageable kind of crappiness, and I am still in good spirits.

Barb was up early this morning, eager to spend time near the water to watch the bathers and also to submerge a few small treasures in the Ganges. Being more interested in sleep, I gave her my necklace to immerse in the river for me—a tiny gold charm with an image of the Christ the Redeemer statue in Rio de Janeiro. "I brought this back from Brazil," said the woman who sold it to me ten years earlier. "It will protect you." I'd decided to believe her on the spot, and the necklace had since become my go-to talisman for travel. Submerging it in the Ganges felt like an appropriate ritual for something I'd worn close to my heart all over the world.

After breakfast, we have a couple hours before we have to make our way to the airport, and we set out to do some last-minute shopping. We follow the route we took with Dinesh on the way to the Golden Temple, where we'd passed a few small shops and vendors selling brass statuettes, copper bowls, and hand-painted figures of Hindu gods small enough to tuck into our suitcases without too much fuss. After working our way through the unavoidable negotiation process that accompanies nearly every purchase in India, Barb and Kolleen decide to return to our hotel. Jennette and I meander a bit longer, then start to make our way back as well. We take our final walk along the Ganges arm in arm, deep in conversation, phones safely tucked in our bags. We need nothing but each other's company amidst the early morning crowds.

Our departure from Varanasi begins with a boat ride, of course, which we get to enjoy beneath the expanse of relatively clear skies. As we pull away from the steps, a group is readying for a dip in the river. The colors and patterns on the women's saris are brighter than a garden in full bloom—gold, orange, turquoise, bright purple, pink, and navy blue with trim the shape of peacock feathers and lotus flower prints. A boat full of thirty or so visitors, all Indian, drifts toward us, and when I hold up my camera in their direction and wave, they oblige with hands in the air and big smiles. We pass a *ghat* covered with huge blocks of white fabric and a pink building accentuated with scalloped archways and pointed spires that look like giant frosted cupcake toppers.

All this time I am thinking about India and the unfathomable truth of how indelibly it has made its mark on me. By the end of this trip, I will have only been in this country for a grand total of thirty-one days. Considering this day marks my 18,330th day on earth, thirty-one days are hardly worth mentioning. Yet something grabbed hold of me the first moment I landed here and has only tightened its grip, even though my experiences this time have already proved far more challenging and disconcerting than the previous one.

As this thought rolls around in my mind, we come to the end of our boat ride and head toward a *ghat* that isn't nearly as steep as all the others. I see a man who looks to be guiding two water buffalo toward the river. When he gets them in, he splashes water on them and rubs them down with his hands. I ask the driver of our boat if the water buffalo belong to the man, and he responds in the affirmative. I can't take my eyes off them—these two massive creatures the color of espresso with curled horns and somber faces; and the man with dark skin and a pot belly who wears only a pink-and-gray-checked cloth around his waist. I know I could easily cry, but I keep the tears at bay. While I fight the infection that is rapidly sinking its claws into my sinuses, I want to avoid having to blow my nose any more than I already am as I survey a scene that feels slightly unbelievable yet entirely obvious. Of course there is a man washing his water buffalo in India. This makes perfect sense.

Although two of us are sick, we all have mixed feelings about leaving Varanasi. The thought of getting away from the big-city pollution and overwhelm we've been dealing with in Delhi and Varanasi is a welcome thought, but there is also something deeply magical and mystical about this city on the river that we are reluctant to leave. In an email I send to my family, I explain that Varanasi is "the most intense, unsettling, life affirming, overwhelming, disturbing and miraculous place I've ever been." It is a place that has me in awe of all the ways the residents of this earth express, embody, and act on behalf of their faith. The thread of God's presence is woven in and around every square inch of Varanasi.

As the four of us take our last lazy ride along the Ganges, I know I will say goodbye to this city with only one word in my heart: *more*. I want more, of everything.

Later on, somewhere between being transfixed by the man washing his water buffalo, a delayed flight out of Varanasi, and a last-minute change of plans that resulted in a five-hour drive from Delhi to Samode Village, I begin to piece it together—the tears and the affection, the reverence and the wonderment. I love India for its sights and sounds and colors, of course, but its hold on me has more to do with the way it enables me to draw closer to my faith and to God, a feat made possible precisely because it is so far from home and so foreign.

India invites me to be with what *is*—with the filth, the cough, and the difficulties inherent in something as simple as needing a bottle of water. It is with the joy of the pilgrims that fill the steps leading down to the Ganges to bathe in what they consider to be their mama, while a few *ghats* down, bodies burn day and night. This is their love and their faith, that they are willing to travel for miles, maybe with the body of someone they love deeply, to be amongst the throngs of other people doing the same thing. These things they do are physically uncomfortable—assaulting, even—and yet they do them without question. Whatever level of ease or hardship any of them might endure in their day-to-day lives, they show up in service to their beliefs and devotions and traditions.

Everywhere I turn, I see and hear expressions of faith: offerings of flowers at the feet of small shrines, the Muslim call to prayer, candles floating on the Ganges, bindis on women's foreheads, and *Qawwali* singers in a twinkle-light-festooned courtyard. I've seen Christian churches, the largest mosque in India, Sikh and Jain temples, Buddhist pilgrimage sites, and countless Hindu shrines. Of the things I've only read about, there are Jain nuns who eat only one meal per day, shamans who memorize and perform four-thousand-line Rajasthani poems, and devotees of the goddess Tara who embed the entrances to their homes with human skulls. Even all the cows I see hold religious significance, as they are worshipped by Hindus. As the providers of life-sustaining milk, they are sacred, seen as maternal figures and symbols of "the divine bounty of earth," one source says. Ayurveda originated in India, and so did yoga. If my aim was to turn away from India's spiritual soul, it would take a determination on par with trying to ignore the snow outside my window in February.

I prayed the day I flew halfway around the world to be here, and I've prayed every day since. I left my tiny bundle of salt, lavender, and stone in the Ganges, and I found comfort in God's presence on the flight from Varanasi to Delhi, when my illness grew to its worst and I felt like a needle was being drilled into my eardrum. Despite the level of physical misery on that ninety-minute flight, it wasn't possible for my prayers to be about anything other than gratitude. *Thank You for keeping me safe. Thank You for my friends, who just provided a packet of tissues. Thank You for the bottle of water that has just been handed to me.* This time around in India, everything hits me more acutely, seeping into my pores and getting beneath my skin. But the challenges I face take place within a vast spiritual universe that keeps showing me I am not alone in my desire to be one with my Creator—God.

It is my very discomfort and the humility it brings that has me so willing to receive everything that is being offered to me right now. However I can, I choose to see all of it as a gift, especially anything asks me to confront and release any picture-perfect façade I might be trying to present to the world. Any opportunity I have to peel back the layers and defenses that separate me from the rest of the world—to be vulnerable, messy, imperfect—I open myself up to the deepest spiritual connections and most profound intimacies.

My mind drifts back to Dinesh and the words he shared with us repeatedly during our time together in Varanasi: "Doubt is in the mind. And faith is in the heart." There are so many ways to interpret this, but right here, right now, what it means for me is this: all of this beauty, discomfort, awe, sensory bombardment, and energy is exactly as it should be.

I do not doubt for one moment that every single molecule of this trip holds a purpose and a gift. I do not doubt the daily suffering that most people on this planet endure or that I have not a single clue what it is like to live with that day to day. And I do not doubt that even in all of this, there is real joy—radiance, even—and that at the root of it is *love*. These people love their Ganges; they love their families; they love their Krishna. And those water buffalo? That man loves them with all of his heart.

Ganga Aarti offerings

Brought forward

Largest Major Rivers

Indus: 1976 miles long, runs
through Pakistan and northern
India

Brahmaputra: 1800 miles long,
originates in southwest Tibet

Main topographical
features of India:

Ganges: 1560 miles long, the
largest river that flows within
India's borders

Himalayan Mountains
(northernmost)

Godavari: 910 miles long, starts
near the Arabian Sea and empties
into the Bay of Bengal

Northern Plains
(northeast)

Indian Desert
(northwest)

Peninsular Plateau
(central/
southcentral)

Latitude: 21.7679°

Longitude: 78.8718°

Coastal Plains
(southern
peninsula)

Highest mountain peak:

Islands
(east and west
sides of
peninsula)

Kangchenjunga

8586 meters, located
at the border of
India and Nepal
in the Himalayas

JANUARY 17, 2018 *Samode Village*

It is late morning in Samode Village, a tiny enclave forty-two kilometers north of Jaipur, and I just woke up from a deep, nine-hour slumber.

We arrived at our hotel last night close to midnight, after a five-hour drive from Delhi that felt otherworldly in a dusty, Mad Max kind of way. Being as sick and exhausted as we were, Jennette and I had crawled into the back seat of our car while Barb and Kolleen got situated in theirs (the only leg of our trip that had us in two separate vehicles), and we promptly closed our eyes for the long haul. As we made our way through the stop-and-go traffic moving out of Delhi, I drifted into a state of consciousness that wasn't quite asleep but definitely wasn't awake.

Considering we were well past normal rush hour, the traffic activity seemed inordinately lively. All the split-second snapshots my mind took each time I opened my eyes showed cars in front of us, trucks alongside us, and the red glare of taillights everywhere. How many times I actually had the level of consciousness needed to retain anything I saw is questionable, so I'm not certain I can trust the hazy memories that linger in my mind this morning. But still, I feel grateful I was too exhausted to feel anxious or worried during last night's frenetic drive.

Our road trip from Delhi was not part of the original plan, but a flight delay out of Varanasi meant a missed connection to Jaipur. It was a blessing, really, the delay. It saved me from having to endure another block of time at thirty thousand feet, where the pressure in my sinuses felt like a vise behind my eyes. I spent much of the flight to Delhi feeling miserable but offering up prayers of gratitude for the delay. I was grateful for the knowledge that once we returned to the ground, we would remain on the ground. That I was able to sleep for most of the drive made me feel like guardian angels were working overtime on my behalf.

What we must have looked like when we arrived beneath last night's canopy of glittering stars. By the time we got here, Barb was sick as well, and after all the delays, the rearrangements, and the long ride in the car, I imagine we stumbled out of our cars like zombies. I remember the way our driver reclined the back seats for Jennette and I and gave us a blanket before we left Delhi—if I could go back and wash that man's feet, I would—but I barely remember being shown to our room. And while I managed to stay calm and level-headed throughout the tumult of our day of travel—a feat made possible, in no small part, by Kolleen's decision to take the reins and arrange for a car from Delhi to Samode once it was clear we would miss our connection, earning her the Badass Merit Badge of the day—I feel like Dorothy in *The Wizard of Oz* after the storm. In Delhi and Varanasi, it was all movement and motion and wildness, but once we arrived here, everything *stopped*.

This morning, it is a revelation to look up and see a clear blue sky, feel the sun on my face, and have the entire space of our hotel's courtyard to myself. While I sit quietly at a table and compose an email to my husband and family about our first week in India, I relish the quietude. I still feel pretty lousy and am managing coughing fits every few minutes, but the ability to sink into a day with no schedule or activities far outweighs my physical discomfort. That I am able to sit still for at least another twenty-four hours feels positively glorious.

As much as I love the unique way Delhi and Varanasi woke me up on every level, this morning I feel weary and raw. Even if I weren't battling a sinus infection, my reserves would be depleted. India is fascinating, life-affirming . . . and *hard*. It has a dark side, as every place does. My thoughts drift back to the night before last, when we returned to our hotel in Varanasi after dark. We passed a mob of people, many of whom were armed with large sticks, getting into a fight. I've encapsulated the memory with a single, overexposed image of a small, sari-clad older woman holding her arms up in front of the crowds as a man approached her from behind and swung a long stick behind his back like a baseball player. At the very instant the man started to move the stick in her direction, our vehicle turned a corner—in that instant, the scene was gone. Did that woman end up getting hit? If so, where was she now? What started the melee in the first place?

It is a scene I will never get out of my mind, when an invisible cloud of rage seemed to consume a group of people for an unknown reason while cars and mopeds zipped by in all directions. In India, at night especially, it is hard to fathom where so many people are going, how they all stay safe, and where they will ultimately rest their heads.

Though I fancy myself game for anything (I rode a bicycle through Delhi, for goodness' sake!), my deepest longing at the moment is for home, even though I am still adjusting to where that longing should be directed. While the actual house I live in now is in Milwaukee, my heart also reaches out toward Santa Barbara and the life my husband and I created there for sixteen years. About a year ago, we started having serious conversations about moving to Wisconsin, and now we are all moved in and just celebrated our first Christmas there. But I don't yet feel firmly rooted in the Midwest. Sitting here, feeling the pull toward home, I recognize how far this yearning extends. Its tentacles reach across time zones and zip codes to the home I live in now as well as the one I recently left.

The day we moved, the movers showed up at about eight in the morning, backed a fifteen-foot truck into our driveway, and went to work. While they carried boxes and furniture out of our house, my husband and I taped up the last cartons, packed suitcases, and prepared the car and trailer for our journey across the country.

In the midst of this flurry of activity, something else was happening. One by one, our neighbors, close friends, and family stopped by our house, many offering gifts of donuts, coffee, and goodie bags filled with treats and mementos from Santa Barbara. With every visitor, we stopped what we were doing and sat with our beloveds. And when the time came to say goodbye, all of us did our best to do it with a smile.

While every one of our visitors that day made it clear they did not want us to move, their love for us was such that they managed to send us off not laden down by guilt and remorse but on wings of joy—with gratitude for having had the time we'd had, for all the new experiences our move would create for us, and for the bittersweet gift of such a deep love. With every visit and ensuing farewell, I felt my heart split open and release a flurry of memories that flew into the air like fireflies.

We'd dared to love each other as deeply as we could—to cry, laugh, eat, celebrate, argue, travel, and pray together. We'd opened our homes to each other, fed each other, and supported each other through divorces, financial meltdowns, and health issues. We'd counseled, encouraged, and comforted each other again and again and again. Would we have given as much and loved as deeply if we'd known my husband and I would eventually make this leap? Absolutely, yes. Did this make our saying goodbye to each other that much harder and heartbreaking? Without question.

As I sit in this open, brightly lit courtyard in a Rajasthani village, I long for a word to describe the day I had to leave all of that, a day that was the most heartbreaking and, at the same time, the most deeply joyful. Never in my life had both of these emotions swirled together so seamlessly, rendering me unable to see where one ended and the other began. But as much as the wordsmith in me wants to find a tidy label for that day—an insignia I can point to and say, "This is what I'm talking about"—I know these efforts are futile.

It isn't possible to distill all of the emotions of that day into a single form; it's the same way I can't quite explain what home means to me at this exact moment, when I am halfway around the world from all the places I've ever lived (now totalling thirty-five). All I know is that I am moving through a familiar current in my desire for what feels safe and familiar—the sound of my husband's voice, my own bed, the cardinals and finches that populate the bird feeder outside our kitchen window.

On every trip I've taken, particularly the ones without my husband, there is always—*always*—a moment when the idea of stopping in my tracks and heading right back home jolts me like a splash of cold water. It isn't because I'm not enjoying where I am or that I'm unable to appreciate the experiences I'm having (something that is especially potent here in India). It's a sudden awareness that as much as I love seeing and learning about other parts of the world—a passion I've had since I was a teenager—nothing comes close to the life I have at home, wherever home happens to be. Of all the gifts I've received in the form of memories and experiences around the globe, they pale in comparison to a boring night at home with my husband. At the end of every trip, returning home to him is always my most treasured reward.

After our time in Varanasi, where up to a hundred people a day go to stand watch as the bodies of their loved ones burn, the reality that he and I have a finite amount of time together looms large. That finiteness is a mystery; it could arrive in a week, or it might not knock on our door for twenty years. It shares a thread of similarity to our move to Wisconsin in the way the idea of relocating hovered in our conversations for years—my husband's longing for home had been an undeniable reality for almost as long as I'd known him—but never felt entirely real until the day we made the decision to do it. Even then, and even despite the fact that we have, in fact, moved, there is some part of me—no bigger than an eyelash—that hasn't quite accepted it, that wonders if we might wake up one day and simply *go back*.

Will I cling to my past in the same way if my husband leaves this earth before I do? In the face of such dramatic and unassailable vicissitude, will such gripping, slight as it may be, haunt me? Torture me? Comfort me?

I think about the notion of living life to the fullest and how different circumstances and experiences have altered what it means to me. I realize it is entirely possible that between our move to Wisconsin and this trip to India, this definition is undergoing yet another a transformation. I feel a pause in my heart, one that has me contemplating something I would have once thought unfathomable: What if this is it? What if I decide to put aside my pursuit of exotic passport stamps in favor of more stillness and rootedness? Is it still true that I need to be a stranger in a strange land to feel like I'm living life to the fullest? Now that we are embarking on a grand new adventure, one that has us relying on each other in ways we've never had to before, what could possibly be more meaningful than that?

I remind myself that no decisions or declarations need to be made as I sit here watching the bubbles in my sparkling water swim to the top of my glass and pop. As I ponder how my internal compass might be reorienting itself while in India, I take another sip of water. It is cold and refreshing, a welcome sensation on my sore throat. I am content to just be, to enjoy a day ahead of me to do what is most needed: to rest, to dream about home, and to be happy.

The day continues to unfold lazily; I move about the estate at the pace of a sloth. I spend time in the hotel's steam room and explore the 475-year-old property, with ballrooms that once held glittering banquets and sumptuous buffets for royalty. Rooms are covered from floor to ceiling with intricate, hand-painted renderings of peacocks, lotus flowers, leaves, and curlicues. In one room the embellishments are all turquoise; in the next room they are a deep mustard yellow; the room after that is royal blue. I find mirrored mosaics, miniature paintings of princes, and scenes depicting lovers strolling through gardens.

Later on, I run into Jennette in the main courtyard. She'd also found the hotel's steam room and, like me, relished the relief it provided to her congestion and sinus pain. She tells me Barb is still in bed, now

with a full-blown fever, and Kolleen, the only healthy one among us, is wandering around on her own. We talk quietly about the challenges of our first days in India and the unexpected longing, as Jennette says, "to simply go home and be in love."

We make our way to the hotel's restaurant and have a light lunch. It is three o'clock by now, and we've barely made it in time to fill a plate from the buffet before it is closed for the day. While slowly consuming lentil soup and buttered *naan*, we agree right then and there to order room service for dinner, a decision mainly motivated by our desire to avoid exposing other hotel guests to our coughing fits. Once this is established, we wonder if it is possible to watch a movie on the TV in our room.

After lunch, we head back to the main courtyard and approach the front desk with our inquiry about movie rentals. The response is an enthusiastic, "Of course!" and we are handed a list of available DVDs. We choose the movie *Traffic*, and it is delivered to our room within minutes.

We spend the next couple of hours puttering about our room. I organize my suitcase, take a bath, and check for messages from my husband on my phone. Kolleen stops by to see how we are doing and shares an update that Barb is feeling slightly more energetic. The two of them have decided to eat dinner in the main courtyard, which is just below our rooms. Not long after, the sound of their voices drifts up through our windows, intermingled with the *ploppity-plop* gurgle of the fountain. As tempting as it is to go outside and enjoy a meal beneath the twinkle lights and stars, I am content to remain in our room, not to mention my pajamas.

After dinner, Jennette and I insert the DVD into the player. When we hit play, the screen is fuzzy and there is no sound. We call the front desk and are told they'll send someone up. It is, at this time, about 7:30.

A diminutive man wearing the hotel uniform—bright purple tunic, pressed pants—shows up at our room within minutes and proceeds to get to work. This involves him taking the two cords connecting the TV to the DVD player and trying every possible combination of cords and plugs possible, all to no avail, while Jennette and I watch.

Watching him puzzle over the fuzzy screen, I realize we've wandered into a scenario I've experienced countless times in India, where the determination to fulfill whatever request is being made becomes immutable, even to the point of offering something that, in the end, may or may not—or, in some cases, can't possibly—be given. Jennette and I are witnessing a pattern that is familiar to me, one that has shaped my characterization of Indians as people who are eager to be helpful, to assist, and to provide whatever it is you need.

I am reminded of an exchange Barb and I had in a hotel in Ranthambore four years ago when her request for a glass of champagne ended up giving us a story we've told dozens of times since.

Barb, to waiter: Do you have champagne?
Waiter: Yes.
Barb: Great! I would like a glass of champagne.
Waiter, after a brief pause: I'm sorry, we don't have.

I've experienced this exact tête-à-tête on numerous occasions on both trips, whereby a request is made to, say, a waiter or a tour guide or someone else responsible for taking care of us in some way. Their immediate answer is yes, but after a bit back and forth, we come to the real answer, which is, as it happens, oftentimes no.

Conversely, we have been taken care of in plenty of moments when it was inconvenient for a person to accommodate us. In Varanasi, when the four of us walked into our hotel just after three in the afternoon, which was listed as the closing time for the lunch service, we gently asked the waiters cleaning up in the dining room if it was possible to order something even though we were late. Without hesitation, they held out their arms toward a table and said, "Yes, of course, come sit down."

I have a hard time believing these automatic yeses are merely the result of hospitality training. Maybe I'm romanticizing it, but there is something undeniably consistent in these wholehearted affirmations and the way we have to wind our way around each other to get to the real answer. It is an exchange that is just as much about wanting to provide whatever we request as it is about wanting or needing to adhere to another plan or arrangement that has already been made.

The impression I have is more of the latter—that it is important our requests be heard and considered (and, in a way, dangled in front of us like a piece of chocolate) but that, in the end, we are going to have to abide by their word, whether out of necessity (hey, if you don't have champagne, you don't have champagne) or their convenience.

But any time there is a possibility a request *can* be fulfilled, efforts will be made to their fullest extent. It is this particular experience Jennette and I are now in, and I know this for certain as soon as our guy leaves our room, explaining he'll be right back. There is no doubt in my mind he will not return alone.

Fast forward to around 8:15, and there are now two DVD players and three purple-tunic-attired gentlemen in our room, all focused on the TV equipment. I am half-asleep as Jennette double checks she's on schedule with the small army of medications at her bedside, prescribed by the doctor who'd visited her earlier in the day.

I know we could try letting them off the hook. We could say, "Don't worry, we don't need to watch a movie," but I'm pretty certain they would ignore us. I imagine them nodding in affirmation only to turn back to the task at hand, not because they are jerks but because they have been assigned a job and will tackle that job with all they have.

I find their determination reassuring. India might shove me out of my comfort zone in ways no other part of the world does, but it has also shown me what it is to be gracious, inviting, and accommodating. I've experienced some of these kindnesses enough that they now feel familiar, and in that recognition I don't feel quite so far out of my element. As I watch them work, I sink more deeply into my pillow, knowing there is nothing I want to change about this moment, that everything is exactly as it should be.

And then, as if by magic, the movie starts playing. The men nod to us quietly before they shuffle out. Benicio del Toro appears on the screen against an overexposed backdrop of Mexican desert, and Jennette and I nestle in for the night.

SARASVATI

Sarasvati is the Hindu goddess of knowledge, music, art, and wisdom. She is worshipped in India as well as Japan, Myanmar, Cambodia, and Tibet. She embodies knowledge and also the highest experience of reality.

JANUARY 18, 2018 *Deogarh*

My second morning in Samode is peaceful and quiet. The four of us decide not to be in a rush for the five-hour drive to Deogarh, our next stop, which enables me—all of us, really—to linger a little longer in this small patch of tranquility.

I start my day back in the hotel's steam room. Spending time there is like resting in a watery cocoon that turns my pores into open, thirsty receptors. Even with Samode's clear atmosphere, my body continues to feel hard against the air around me. It is as if all the cells of my skin have arranged themselves to prevent anything from getting in or out, perhaps in response to my body's lost battle with the elements in the first part of our trip. But in the steam room, all those defense mechanisms melt away. I can, for once, breathe normally. The coughing fits are less frequent.

After the steam, I bundle myself up in a thick white robe, walk out to the hotel's pool, and lie down on a lounge chair facing the sun. The golden warmth of the sun prickles my cheeks and serves as a perfect punctuation mark at the end of the brief respite Samode has provided from movement and activity. *If I could just stay here one more day*, I think, *maybe this illness would go away*. It is a thought that lands delicately in my mind, like a butterfly gently moving its wings back and forth, practically taunting me. I know it's not possible to alter our plans, but I linger with the thought nonetheless. *Sleep, steam, sun*, I imagine, *for just one more day.*

After returning to our room and getting myself ready for today's journey, the morning continues to unfold peacefully. I wander around the property, have breakfast, and buy a white embroidered cotton tunic in the hotel's gift shop. The four of us convene in the main courtyard just before noon, settle up our charges with the hotel, and make our way to our van. The brief respite we've enjoyed in Samode Village is over; today we go to Deogarh.

I tend not to do a lot of research before I travel. I might learn about and put a few things on a must-see list, but my preference is to make discoveries more organically. This approach has served me well, providing me with spontaneity and surprises instead of checklists and agendas.

Because the prime planning period for this trip coincided with my move to Wisconsin, my role in the decision-making process was peripheral at best. My contribution, for the most part, didn't amount to much more than, "Sounds great!" or "Looks good!" When Barb suggested we put a visit to Deogarh on our itinerary, I didn't look it up, google it, or ask why she'd landed on that particular point on the map of Rajasthan. I just tossed her my usual nugget of affirmation like a piece of popcorn and turned my attention back to my storage unit in Milwaukee.

Deogarh sits inside a triangle formed by Jaipur, Jodhpur, and Udaipur, three popular tourist destinations Barb and I visited in 2014. Our hotel is situated on the edge of the main town and is owned by a couple who exude Indian hospitality and sophistication. They speak impeccable English with the perfect whiff of a British accent, her voice a measured yet confident tone and his energetic and excitable. Her oval face, long nose, and simple red bindi feature prominently against her long, dark hair pulled back in a low bun, and each day she wears beautifully woven saris. Her husband has a full head of dark hair flecked with gray; his boyish face makes it easy to imagine what he might have looked like as a twelve-year-old.

As our time here unfolds, a picture begins to form in my mind of the quality and intelligence of their intentions. Nothing is arbitrary, and during our visit I experience repeated waves of mild sadness that my energy is compromised. If I was feeling healthy and invigorated, I would be able to engage with the experiences they have created for us. Instead, I have to settle for being more of an observer than a full participant.

Our evening begins in the courtyard around a fire pit with the hotel guests and the owners. Everyone is introduced to an older woman seated across from me, who, it turns out, is the husband's mother. I learn there is a steady flow of family members in and out of the hotel—something I say about my own home. One family member left yesterday; the woman in front of me, the husband's mother, will be here until tomorrow. On that day, we will meet their niece.

Most everyone enjoys a glass of wine while I have sparkling water. It is not yet seven, and I am already feeling the call to sleep. (Barb, back to feeling miserable, headed straight to bed when we arrived, and I haven't seen her since.)

But this gathering seems part of the routine of this hotel and of the owners' vision. I can sense this ritual speaks to the importance they place on the art of conversation and international communion. People from all walks of life and many corners of the world gather, talk, and receive snippets of insight, advice, or encouragement. This has happened at other places we've visited—a lovely woman from the United Kingdom at our hotel in Samode gave Jennette and me a few packets of LemSip, a cold remedy from her country, when she learned we were sick—but the evening here in Deogarh has been arranged for the express purpose of creating these kind of exchanges.

We make our way to the dining room before too long, where one long table is covered with various cotton woodblock-printed table covers. A multi-course meal is served, each dish presented to us individually by a small team of servers. The dishes are simple and unusual—carrot soup seasoned with cinnamon, chickpea stew, and warm, buttery *naan*. We are dining with hotel guests from the United Kingdom and Germany who regale us with stories from their travels in other parts of India. On most days I would take notes and offer my own travel-related tidbits in a conversation like this, but tonight I am tired. As soon as dinner is finished, I say good night and head straight to bed.

The list of today's excursions is short—only two options. That they are both relatively passive activities is just fine with me, and they also sound like a lot of fun. In the morning, we will go on what is described as a "rural rail ride," and sometime later in the day we can take an open-air Jeep ride through the provincial outskirts of the main village.

Our travel agent did an especially good job describing the train ride, and I have been looking forward to it since I first read about it in our trip outline:

> Explore a marvelous rural ride that pays great homage to the past as well as providing transportation for locals. This authentic experience allows you to travel through the stunning tranquil countryside through viaducts and into forested areas on a classic 1930s meter gauge train! As you chat with the other friendly and inquisitive passengers, pass through quaint bygone railway stations that offer you a most wonderful experience of vintage travel.

I still don't feel great, but I'm on the mend. Jennette is more upbeat than she has been since Varanasi, Barb is getting up and about slowly, and the grin that came across Kolleen's face the day we landed in India is still going strong. We might be a little worn around the edges, but we're all in high spirits and ready for the day's adventure.

We drive from the hotel to the train station with today's tour guide, Mukesh, who looks to be in his late twenties. He's a little taller than I am and lean, with a chatty nature and an easy smile. We arrive at the train station early, which gives us time to take in the scene slowly.

The station is not desolate but sparsely occupied. A few small children huddle near two British couples close to the tracks. The children hold out their hands with plaintive expressions every few minutes, while a stray blond puppy lingers at their feet. Close by, an older man wearing a white collared shirt, white pants, and a gray knit cap squats in front of a large metal bowl. Inside the bowl, meticulously arranged, are his lunch-time offerings for sale. A small stack of newspapers clusters in a bundle on the far side of the bowl. Closest to him, lined up inside the bowl along the edge, from about four o'clock to eight o'clock, are five perfectly ripe tomatoes. In between is a blend of chopped vegetables and a bright orange jar of spices. These kind of makeshift food stalls are ubiquitous in India. Bowls, trays, and carts display rice, vegetables, chickpeas, and other items, which are scooped up and packaged in sheets of newspaper coiled in the shape of a cone. The train station is this man's territory; he is here to feed hungry travelers.

At one point, I watch a large dog begin to approach the puppy from a few yards away. When the puppy yelps, a few other even larger dogs bolt in from out of nowhere to chase the offending dog away. There is clearly a canine hierarchy at the train station, one that does not bode well for any dog looking to challenge the status quo.

Something can be said for time spent watching the world go by—or, in this case, watching people sit still and wait for the next train. When it does finally arrive and passengers wrapped in colorful shawls and flip-flops disembark, I think about the timeless nature of trains and train stations—how, depending on what part of the world I'm in, they've conjured dreamy imaginings of times long past and also provided a glimpse of what the world might look like in the future.

My first trip to another continent was singularly defined by trains and by seeing another part of the world from the vantage of a rail car. The European rail system made it possible for me to immerse myself in everything from the French Impressionists in Paris to Gaudi's curvy architectural wonders in Barcelona to the reunification of East and West Germany. (I wasn't there when the wall came down, but I was there the day they officially merged back together, when celebrations the likes of Oktoberfest took place under enormous tents just beyond the border in East Germany.)

Years later, when I was able to tag along with my husband on his business trips to Tokyo, I saw the countryside of Japan whiz by at two hundred miles per hour on the bullet train. Whenever I saw it pull into a station, all sleek milky gloss and with a nose as pointed as a dolphin's, I felt like I'd just been transported into a science-fictionalized future. I love trains for the very fact that they get travelers where they need to go at a pace that, while still far beyond that of our ancient human ancestors, with their horse-drawn covered wagons and camel caravans, is more human. As a twenty-two-year-old backpacker, I could board a train in Paris and watch the way the landscape changed, hour by hour, as I made my way to Munich.

I don't know anything about today's excursion beyond the basic fact of our taking a train ride, but that is enough for me. I board the train expecting a time of quiet repose that allows me to sit by a window and admire the scenery as we roll through the countryside. But the mood and energy take an immediate and unexpected turn as soon as we board. Once the train starts moving, the fun begins.

The ride is an exuberant and sometimes comical exercise in international diplomacy—not to mention an informal photo shoot for any local passenger willing to let us take their picture. Most people are happy to oblige; I take photos of older men and women, a shy teenager, a mother and son, and group selfies. One young man jumps back and forth between all four of us to pose and take selfies. Wearing a blue chambray shirt and jeans, he has thick wavy hair, sideburns, and a wide moustache that he pauses to carefully curl up at the edges like a nineteenth-century cowboy before any of us takes a picture of him. His face is expressive and playful as he preens for an assortment of photos. He even plays the role of art director, situating me inside one of the seating compartments and then leaning out of the train's open doorway so I can take his picture through the window.

Mukesh, who is seated in one of the compartments with four other passengers, asks me to join him at one point. I sit down between him and another man who is the Indian version of Keith Richards, minus the dangly earrings. The man's attire is all beige—beige tunic, light beige pants, striped beige scarf wrapped around his head. His neck is adorned with multiple necklaces that have large gold charms, and he wears mirrored sunglasses. He has razor stubble, full lips, and a head of cropped salt-and-pepper hair mussed to look as if he'd just rolled out of bed. Later, when I'm looking through all the photos, I will discover him in the background of a picture I took of Kolleen and the young man with the curly moustache. His sunglasses are off, and I notice that his entire right eyeball is milky white, as if it was dipped in bleach.

As soon as I sit down, the Indian Keith Richards begins holding court, talking boisterously, waving his hands for effect, and cracking up everyone, most especially himself. Mukesh is particularly tickled by the man's jokes; he laughs loudly, punctuating each howl with a single clap of the hands. In between fits of laughter, he tries to explain to me what the other man is saying, but I'm only able to grab every fourth word or so. It isn't enough to understand exactly what the punch line is, but it's enough to figure out I somehow play into what makes the stories so outrageous and comical. (The other hint is the way everyone looks at him while he speaks, then moves their attention to me when they laugh. This, in and of itself, makes me chuckle.)

I may be the punch line of a joke, but I'm okay with that because everyone is having such a good time. As Mukesh continues trying to interpret, Kolleen walks by and asks what's going on. I look at her from within this small huddle of locals and tell her, above the noise of the group, that I have no idea what's happening. She smiles, shakes her head, and keeps moving toward the other compartments, continuing her joyful meanderings and exchanges with the locals.

Kolleen has taken me completely by surprise on this trip. She was the last of the four of us to commit to our plans, having had the most concerns about how she would fare with the intensities of India. While Barb and Jennette couldn't wait to hit the go button, Kolleen admitted she was looking for a reason to say no—some sign from God or the universe or her daughter's volleyball schedule. I'd had numerous conversations with her during the months leading up to our trip, not only to talk through her misgivings, but also to impart what I felt deep in my bones—that Kolleen's heart, already deeply sensitive and spiritual, was going to be cracked open in ways she couldn't imagine. That she harbored fears over whether or not she had the strength and stamina to absorb all the energy of India only reinforced my intuitive hit that she, perhaps more than any of us, needed to go.

Which is why I can't help but want to laugh at the formidable, unexpected confidence and delight she has embodied from the moment we arrived, most especially in light of how physically wrecked Barb, Jennette, and I have been for most of our time here. I had confidence in my friend's ability to move through the wild waters of this part of the world, but she is riding through these rapids with the ease and strength of a daredevil kayaker. Kolleen was concerned this environment would be too much for her; turns out, instead, that she's found her element—one that is raw, messy, and intrinsically human.

I feel giddy as the train comes to a complete stop at the station, and also disappointed the ride is over. I think about an afternoon spent at one of the East Coast's major amusement parks when I was twelve years old, when sparse crowds allowed the roller coaster's operator to offer the small gaggle of kids I was part of repeated rides, one after another. Every time the roller coaster pulled into the station, the operator would slow down our speed, yell, "Again?" and receive our wholehearted yes before sending us back on our way.

This is what I want right now. I want to lean my head out the window, where I'll see the station master and hear him yell, "Again?" so I can scream yes at the top of my lungs. It is that longing, the same one I had after Varanasi, the longing for *more*.

My friends and fellow passengers have become a merry band of rabble rousers on this loop around the countryside—laughing, telling stories, posing for pictures, and stopping from time to time to admire the langur monkeys hanging around the railroad tracks in hopes of a snack. We couldn't speak each other's language, and we knew we would never see each other again, but we carried on nonetheless, almost as if old friends—which, some might say, especially in India, where a large swath of the population believes in reincarnation, we might have been. From their perspective, it wouldn't even be a question. "We've known each other before," they'd say, "and we'll find each other again—in a different form, another lifetime, or maybe in a heavenly realm."

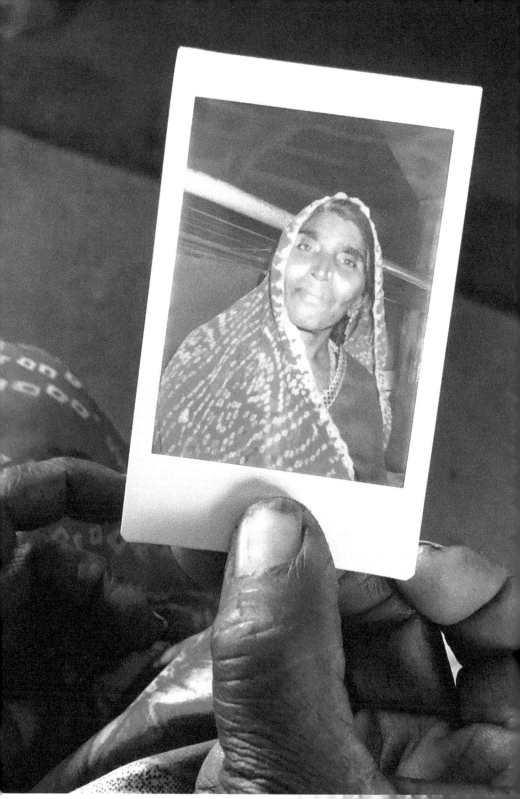

JANUARY 20, 2018 *Treasure Hunt*

Jennette and I have risen early for our last morning in Deogarh. We will leave soon after breakfast for today's drive to Agra, so if the two of us want to accomplish the mission we set for ourselves yesterday, we need to be out the door and on our way before eight. We don't need any encouragement to make this happen; we know our efforts will be rewarded.

After we returned from the train ride yesterday, Mukesh took us on a walk through the village of Deogarh, and we discovered an antique shop the size of a walk-in closet. Its shelves were covered with an assortment of objects and relics: brass animal figures; scrolls of smooth paper the color of tea; trays filled with buttons; stacks of brass bowls; beaded bracelets; ceramic drawer knobs; aged illustrations of Hindu gods; and mounds of vintage fabrics, knits, and quilted pieces. For the two of us, it was the mother lode, and we settled in for a long, relaxed treasure hunt.

Too quickly, Mukesh leaned into the store and announced we needed to leave in order to be back to the hotel in time for our Jeep ride, which Barb did not want to miss. The owner of the shop, an older gentleman with glasses and a gray moustache, told us not to worry; he would be open at eight the next morning. While being rushed out the door, we gave him our emphatic promise we would return in the morning at eight on the nose. This morning, as our agreed-upon time approaches and the sun continues its ascent into the clouds, we aim to follow through with our promise.

The owners of the hotel know about our plans and insist on sending us into the village with a guide, who turns out to be a young, soft-spoken man who has assisted in the serving of meals and also leads yoga classes at the hotel. We follow the same route we took with Mukesh, believing we'll turn a corner and find our wee antique shop with lights ablaze and the owner beckoning us forward. Instead we face rows of unopened shops with a few lone pigeons pecking about. Although

Jennette and I recognize a couple small landmarks, we find ourselves walking in circles, trying to find the shop.

Just as we are about to give up, we notice our impromptu tour guide talking intently with a couple of other gentlemen nearby, one of whom flings open the door to his own shop, wanting us to browse his collection of souvenirs. Within seconds, the other one dials a number on his flip phone and starts talking excitedly. Less than five minutes later, our friendly antique shop owner is walking briskly toward us in what looks like pajama bottoms. It doesn't matter to the other men that this means we'll spend our money somewhere other than their store; the minute they got wind of our dilemma, they sprang into action to help us find what we needed.

Minutes later, Jennette and I begin accumulating our collections of goodies while the shopkeeper, along with his wife, who came down a few minutes later, answers whatever questions we have about his wares.

After all of the items we can't live without—textiles, handwritten scrolls, small brass figures—are wrapped in a bag, the woman, who is shorter than her husband, moves over in order to stand directly in front of us. Wisps of gray fan out from her forehead into her dark hair. She raises her arms at the elbows in order to hold up her hands with her fingers pointing down. With a huge smile on her face, she watches as the realization of what we are looking at hits us: six fingers on both hands.

"And!" she says, motioning downward—six toes on both feet.

Like a proud parent, she details the way the six-digit gene has traveled her family lineage. Her grandmother, mother, brother, and sister have at least one set of six fingers or toes, although most of them are like her, with twenty-four digits total. She beams as she shares these stories, relishing our wide-eyed fascination. I get the feeling she loves springing this detail of her physicality on people, waiting for just the right moment, like a cat ready to pounce on its favorite toy. I imagine her calm anticipation as Jennette and I browsed, considered, and then finally paid for our goods, whereupon she stood up tall and quietly drew our attention toward herself.

As we prepare to leave, I pull out my Polaroid, something I've done sporadically during our trip. I had only one regret from my 2014 visit to India, which was that I didn't bring my Polaroid camera. It is with me this time, along with ten packs of film and a single intention: use up all the film; give most of the photos away.

This might be the single best decision I've made, as the Polaroid camera has invited all kinds of happy exchanges everywhere we've gone. As soon as I bring it out, a magic portal of connection opens that causes a delightful kind of uproar. Once people see it, responses and requests tend to fall on either side of two extremes: some step forward for a brief photo shoot; others don't move a muscle but fix their gaze on me and stare. It is one of the few moments I can, with great confidence, actually read someone's mind. When I respond by holding up the camera and offering an inviting nod of my head, I receive a subtle nod back and then step forward to take the photo.

I have to get fairly close to each subject in order for the photo to look decent. I also have to instruct each person where to look for the camera. It takes a few tries to get this routine figured out after a couple photos end up too blurry or overexposed. Some people smile big; others look reticent. One older gentleman with a thick gray moustache and a fuschia pink turban looks positively regal in his photo, while a younger woman with a gold nose ring, perfect skin, and thick, dark hair refuses to smile, despite how clear it is she wants her photo taken. After I take the Polaroid photo, coaxed by her continued stare, I take more photos of her with my phone.

The Polaroids are small—only the size of a credit card—but there's something sweet about offering perfect strangers a gift without it being awkward or overly friendly. At times the person looks taken aback when I hand him or her the photo, but others nearby often clamor to partake.

This morning, as I take the first Polaroid photo of the antique shop owners, our impromptu guide from the hotel gasps when he sees the photo slide out of the camera. As soon as the brief whizzing sound starts, his eyes grow wide and his jaw drops. He is young, maybe twenty-two, and humble—traits I saw in him the moment we were first introduced the day we arrived in Deogarh. His reaction to the Polaroid is the most animated I've seen him.

After taking one more photo of the couple for my own collection, I direct him to stand in front of the shop. I hold up the camera and take his photo, then observe him watching the film emerge. As we make our way back to our hotel while his photo develops, he still seems gobsmacked. He shakes his head in amazement and, tightly grasping his photo on the edge of the film as I'd instructed, declares, "I will never, *ever* forget you."

And just like that, our stories are entwined forever, held together by a photograph and the wonder of modern technology. Jennette and I return to our hotel, slaphappy over the events of our morning, hearts and bags bursting with riches.

Before we leave our hotel in Deogarh, Jennette discovers she left one of her bags of purchases at the antique shop. We confer with the hotel's owner, who starts dialing her phone. After a few conversations, we are told the antique shop closed as soon as we'd left because the owners needed to go out of town for the day.

A plan of action is devised to procure Jennette's package and have it sent to our hotel in Jaipur, but Jennette is despondent. Almost every aspect of this plan seems unlikely—that the hotel's owner will be diligent to get in touch with the shopkeeper with everything else she has to manage, that he'll get the purchases to her in a timely manner, that it will arrive in time for Jennette to receive it in Jaipur.

Once we are on the road, I move up the aisle of our van to Jennette's seat.

"I know you think your package is gone," I say, "but I'm telling you that everyone is going to do whatever they can to get it to you."

I am reminding Jennette of my favorite of all of India's personality traits: their desire to be of service. I see her struggle not to get her hopes up, and I understand why she does this. But as I make my way back to my seat and sit down, I sink into a solid cushion of confidence that she will have the missing treasures in her hands before we leave Jaipur.

Less than forty-eight hours later, it is so.

As Jennette unwraps her beloved prizes, I have only one thought: *Once again, India comes through.*

Shopowners
Deogarh, India

CHAI SPICE MIX

3 tsp cardamom seeds
2 tsp ground ginger
1 tsp ground cinnamon
¼ tsp ground clove
¼ tsp ground black pepper

Mix all ingredients
together well;
store in a jar.

MASALA CHAI

1 tsp chai spice mix
1 ½ cups water
2/3 cup whole milk*
3-4 tsp cane sugar
2 tsp loose leaf Assam tea
   (or other black tea of your choice)

Combine chai spice mix + water in
small saucepan; place over high heat,
bring to a boil. Turn off heat, steep
for 5 min. Turn flame to medium; when
tea begins to simmer, add milk +
sugar, stirring often. When chai
begins to boil, stir in tea leaves
and turn off heat. Cover pot; let tea
sit for 4-5 min. Strain chai into
individual serving cups and enjoy!

*do not use reduced-fat milk

GOLDEN MILK

1 cup whole milk*
½ tsp turmeric powder
¼ tsp ground ginger
¼ tsp ground cardamom
2-3 strands saffron, soaked in
     1 tsp warm water (optional)
Pinch of ground nutmeg (optional)
Honey

Place all ingredients except honey in
small saucepan over medium heat. Whisk
until milk is hot and just begins to
simmer. Pour golden milk into mug. Add
honey to taste.

*or non-dairy milk of your choice

JANUARY 20, 2018 *Truck Stop*

Every truck in India is a work of art on four or more wheels, vibrant with a hodgepodge of embellishments that would make most tween girls swoon: multicolored pom-poms, fluorescent tapes, sparkly mobiles, metallic garland, and rows of plastic reflectors. Truck drivers decorate their vehicles to psychedelic effect with these ornaments, along with hand-painted designs called kitsch. Lotus flowers, cranes, Hindu gods, birds, fish, and tigers—these are just some of the subjects painted on trucks we pass as we drive all over Rajasthan. The trucks also display traffic warnings such as "Blow Horn" and prideful sentiments like "Great India" in a multitude of colors and fanciful typography styles.

After admiring these compositions for nearly two weeks and noticing the dozens of roadside stalls that sell the ornaments and supplies we've seen hanging, bobbing, and swinging on the trucks, we tell our driver we want to stop at one. On this particular day, we are somewhere between Deogarh and Jaipur, and all four of us are in a slightly daffy mood, laughing hysterically at anything we find the least bit funny and talking up a storm about yesterday's train ride. We are all, at the moment, at least moderately healthy, which is likely the driving force behind our excitability. Jennette and I skipped dinner at our hotel last night in favor of golden milk, two hot water bottles, and an early bedtime—which, considering how we feel this morning, looks to have been a smart move.

No sooner do we relay this request to our driver than Jennette exclaims, "There's one!"

With a bemused look on his face, our driver pulls over. The door opens, and out we spill—four blue-eyed women on a mission, dust flying up around us.

We walk toward the stall, which includes an awning-covered area in front of the main "shop." At first glance, it looks like a small storage unit with a table in front and a few rows of shelves holding various trinkets and baubles. Metallic garland and pom-poms the size of baseballs made with dark blue yarn hang along the edges of the awning and sway back and forth with each breeze.

Three gentlemen hold court at the stall. As we look around and begin pointing at the items we want, the youngest of them, who has a faint moustache, clear brown eyes, and a sharp jawline, begins dialing his phone. With a stunned look on his face, he says a few words to the person on the other end and then holds the phone toward us; he has initiated a video call, and we are the stars of the show.

Another man behind the table is all smiles, laughter, and affection; he touches each of us on the head whenever possible. He is wearing a pale orange *shalwar kameez* (light, loose trousers), a tangerine-and-white-checked scarf, and a bright mauve jacket. The tips of the salt-and-pepper hair on his head display scattered tufts of a richer shade of orange that reminds me of persimmon, and this pop of color features prominently on his beard, which reaches about an inch below his chin. No part of his attire, including his mostly orange beard, seems arbitrary. This is a man who appreciates style, who pays attention to the details. When he smiles, which is pretty much constantly, he reveals perfectly straight, white teeth, and his eyes tightly squint. While it seems impossible for the younger man to absorb the scene unfolding in front of him, this man with the orange beard is all too eager to get the most fun out of this that he can. He, too, dials up a friend and has each of us say hello.

I have seen amazing sights while I'm in India, just as I did the first time I came, and I will continue to see them: multi-colored temples on the side of the road; massive, centuries-old forts that loom large over cities; yellow fields of mustard; and, of course, the queen of all landmarks in India, the Taj Mahal. Our itinerary was planned around these sights, in fact—these buildings, places, and structures with rich and impressive histories. And I will go home with hundreds of photos of these monuments, and maybe even a little bit of knowledge about them. But the stories I'll end up telling repeatedly will be of afternoons like yesterday on the train and today, here, by the side of the road. I know the memories that will blaze brightest in my mind will be of the man with the orange beard, the shop owner with six fingers and toes, the Indian Keith Richards, and the woman in Varanasi who had a smile that was my grandma's.

All the great wonders of the world, whether made by human hands or created in nature, have the power to awe and amaze and teach me something about the world I live in. I've stood in a forest of bristlecone pine trees in Northern California, some of which are believed to be more than five thousand years old and the oldest living things on the planet. I've sat in a cathedral in Berlin, half of which remains as it was after World War II: a heap of bombed-out rubble, a somber piece of history in the middle of a modern city. I've walked through the ancient city of Petra in Jordan, which was a thriving community of twenty thousand at its peak in the first century AD. These experiences have been meaningful and at times even brought me to tears.

But what happens with all these places and so many others is that they become a kind of fancy backdrop to the memories and stories of people I've traveled with and met along the way. With all the books and magazine articles that tell readers what they "must" do and see before they die, I wonder if the most meaningful and transformative element of travel—connecting with our fellow humans on other parts of the globe—isn't getting lost in all the top ten (or one hundred or one thousand) lists. The part about diplomacy, and kindness, and respecting a country not merely because it has the buildings we want to see and the natural wonders we want to admire but because it is filled with people trying to do the same things we're trying to do: raise happy children, create a comfortable home, live, love, laugh.

If I were to create my own smaller-scale, human-centric list of travel ambitions, it might look like this:

❧ *Have a conversation with someone from a foreign country about faith.*

❧ *Work in a kitchen that provides free lunches for the community.*

❧ *Meet someone with six fingers and toes.*

❧ *Take a Polaroid photo of a man in a turban.*

❧ *Laugh your head off with perfect strangers, even if you're not sure what you're laughing about.*

It is magnificently easy to fall in love with perfect strangers in India. The same can be said for other parts of the world—anywhere, really—but it is especially true in India, even though we start most exchanges looking at each other like zoo animals. But something soon clicks into place—*Oh, I see you're a human too!*—and a happy pandemonium explodes. With one smile, nod, or head bobble, a door is flung wide open, and any passerby would think we've known each other for years. It's as if we're better able to see our shared humanity because we are, on the outside, so different. We find the differences fascinating at first, and that fascination gives way to a cellular recognition of the truth of what holds us together: our light, our humanity, our divine and miraculous essence.

The media would have me believe the world is a scary place, but I try not to fall down that rabbit hole. There is no denying it is a mess, with problems that seem insurmountable, dispiriting, and, in some cases, yes, terrifying. But any time I go out into the world—whether to my local grocery store or to a roadside stand selling pom-poms for trucks in India—if I'm able to smile and laugh with a stranger, then it can't be all that bad. As long as there are those of us willing to be joyfully surprised and we can somehow find each other, I'll choose to believe there is hope for humanity, that we just might make it after all.

We finalize our purchases and take a few more photos, then climb into the van, elated with our swag. As we slip back into traffic, I want to look at the pictures I've just taken.

I flip through the photos and see him—the mysterious third man. I'm afraid to say I barely noticed him when we were there. With a thick gray moustache that hangs past his lips like a bushy mermaid's tail, he hangs in the background of a photo I took of myself with the orange-bearded man. He looks regal, composed, and very serious. He is far enough behind us in the photo to distort the perspective; his head appears comically, nonsensically small. He is situated precisely between me and the orange-bearded man, making it appear as if his absurdly small head had grown out from between our shoulders.

In an age where photobombing has become a subversive art form, here was this quiet, unassuming gentleman—who played it so cool during our shopping spree, he didn't even register—posing like a king, photobombing like a pro.

JANUARY 20, 2018 *Jaipur Arrival*

Jaipur. Founded on my birth date (so says Wikipedia) on November 18, 1727, and known as the Pink City. It is my second time here, and just like the first time, I have arrived with giddy anticipation.

Awaiting our late-afternoon arrival are Vineeta and Nisha, residents of Mumbai and unlikely friends of mine. Despite our living on opposite sides of the planet, we've managed not only to find each other, but also to collaborate on a book, visit each other on numerous occasions in both of our home countries, and, in the process, build a meaningful friendship—no small accomplishment with a ten-and-a-half-hour time difference between us.

I head down to meet them first, then Jennette, Kolleen, and Barb quickly follow. Once Jennette and Kolleen are introduced, the circle is complete. By the end of dinner, we've formed our own tribe.

Vineeta is an artist, designer, and lifestyle maven with a popular online presence. Our creative pursuits brought us together ten years ago, when she discovered my work through a design blog and then featured me on hers. Having long been fascinated by India and having toyed with the idea of going there for years, I relished the idea of someday meeting a kindred spirit in that part of the world. When I started working on a collaborative book in 2010 about the transformative power of creating a meaningful life, she was at the top of my list of contributors. When the book was released in 2011, she flew to Los Angeles, where I lived at the time, for the launch party.

This is how many of my friendships begin: through digital connections and the wonders of the internet. The narrative of my long-distance friendship with Vineeta runs parallel to the advent of various technologies and platforms, where blogging and email gave way to Instagram,

Skype, and WhatsApp. (We throw the occasional bit of snail mail in there, too, just for good measure.) For as much as I bemoan the way social media has come to consume our collective time and energy, it does have its merits. It enabled Vineeta and me to recognize one another from afar and to keep our connection going year after year. And when Vineeta invited her friend Nisha to join her on the weekend trip she took to Jaipur to spend time with me and Barb in 2014, Nisha was immediately folded in, too, further expanding the universe of our friendship.

Vineeta has one of the most amazing smiles you'll ever see. It radiates joy and is wide in a Julia Roberts kind of way, but Vineeta has slightly fuller lips and longer teeth. I always find it hard to believe how much shorter than me she is; in photos, the top of her head reaches my chin. Her energy and personality—buoyant and colorful, with an easy laugh—makes me imagine her taller.

But it isn't merely her smile, large brown eyes, or dark, curly hair that flows past her shoulders that makes Vineeta stand out. It is the way she flings herself right into the real stuff. With Vineeta, there is no, "How is the weather in Milwaukee?" Instead it's, "Tell me how your move has influenced your creative work," and, "What has it *really* been like to be with your husband in this new way?" She wants to get to the heart of things, to explore the meaning behind our experiences.

In conversations, Vineeta can barrel ahead at full speed with a story, only to notice some tangential thought drift into her line of sight, whereby she immediately and succinctly addresses it. On a recent Skype call, as soon as we'd exchanged hellos, she dove into a discussion about a topic we'd been chatting about through WhatsApp text messages. A few minutes later, she stopped mid-sentence, looked at me, and said, "Oh my god, I just started talking and haven't stopped." Another time, when offering brief background for another story, she abruptly paused and said, "Wait, let's stick to the main topic," wrapped up the background snippet, and returned to her original thought. This is just one way she absorbs and responds to every detail of her surroundings.

Nisha, who is slightly taller than Vineeta, with short, dark hair cropped close at the back of her neck, was more reserved when we met but seemed to relish the curiosity Barb and I had about seemingly mundane details of her life. Whatever questions we had, she answered them thoughtfully, punctuating most of them with one of the most exuberant head bobbles I've seen in all of India. The friendship she shares with Vineeta holds a sweet kind of balance. Whereas Vineeta is an artist who is happy to spend time wandering, Nisha, a brand consultant, is more matter-of-fact and pragmatic. Between these differences in temperament, they share a committed spiritual practice that includes monthly retreats with a guru.

When the four of us—me, Barb, Vineeta, and Nisha—shared a weekend in Jaipur in 2014, we saw some amazing places, but the highlights centered around meals. Between dinner our first night and a long, leisurely lunch the next day, we might as well have been in our own clubhouse. We lost track of time to such an extent during lunch that our tour guide, who was waiting with our driver near the restaurant, started to wonder if we'd gone somewhere else. We were too busy getting lost in each other's worlds—Barb and I hanging on their every word as they described what it is like to live and work in Mumbai; Vineeta and Nisha listening intently as we discussed Barb's work as an artist and mine as a writer. They taught us the proper use of a finger bowl and explained their work as Reiki healers.

By the time we said goodbye on the side of a busy thoroughfare near the Bapu Bazar, one of Jaipur's larger open-air markets, I felt like I'd been given an array of insights about life in India that wouldn't be available in any guidebook or website. Simply by talking about their lives, Vineeta and Nisha opened up a world—one I was eager to get to know.

Right before they climbed into a rickshaw at the end of that first visit, Nisha approached and looked me in the eye. "I'm *so* happy I came," she gushed, a huge smile on her face. After being told earlier that it had taken some coaxing for her to fly from Mumbai to Jaipur to spend a weekend with us—who wouldn't have needed convincing to get on an airplane for perfect strangers?—my shoulders softened at her affection. We hugged goodbye as the traffic whizzed by with its cacophony of engines and horns, and I held one thought in my mind: *I know this won't be the last time I see them. I know we will meet again.*

Given the technological wonders available today, not to mention *airplanes*, I know it isn't outrageous to have friends in other countries. But I still hold a special place of pride and gratitude for the friendship I share with these two women who live halfway around the world. Any number of hurdles could have prevented Vineeta and me from moving beyond being online buddies to real friends, ranging from the administrative and governmental to the more personal and foundational—skin color, family background, faith. It takes effort to keep a friendship vibrant and strong, even if both parties share the same zip code. For Vineeta and me, it would have been all too easy to say, "Hello, it's nice to meet you," in the space of an email message and then go about our business. Instead, we took advantage of the opportunities presented to us to be in touch and to get to know each other.

And now here we are, a decade later, sitting together in the lobby of a hotel in Jaipur, shaking our heads in disbelief. *These are my friends*, I think, *and this is nothing short of a miracle.*

JANUARY 21, 2018 *Jaipur*

Jaipur is a dynamic city but not nearly as big or crowded as Delhi or Varanasi. We've been told by our tour guide that the powers that be set a goal for Jaipur to stand apart from other well-known India tourist destinations with regard to pollution and litter—to clean things up—and I see evidence of this. Walking along the avenues lined with low-slung buildings the color of salmon and burnt peach, I find the sidewalks swept clean and that it's easier to breathe. In Delhi, even the leaves on the trees are covered in dust, but in Jaipur my lungs (and the trees) get a much-needed break.

Our time here will comprise nearly an exact replica of our 2014 visit. We end up with the same tour guide—Vikram—whom Barb and I nearly tackle, we are so excited to see him, and we will visit most of the same sights.

We start with the Palace of Winds and make our way to City Palace, a complex built in the early 1700s. Upon entering a large courtyard, a group of six young women approaches Barb for a group selfie. I begin to document their mini photo shoot, and then Barb and I become magnets. Within minutes, we are surrounded by a large group, around twenty or so, of boys and girls who range in age from sixteen to twenty. Most of the girls wear colorful, patterned saris, shawls, and *shalwar kameezes*; the boys wear polo shirts and hoodies. Many have sunglasses on, and almost all of the girls wear lipstick. One girl asks me how old I am. When I look at her intently and exclaim, "I'm fifty!" her eyes grow wide and her jaw drops, and I wonder what her vision of a fifty-year-old woman is.

A few minutes later, one of the young men directs all of us to stand together for a large group shot, and I walk to the front of the group and hold my arms out wide, as if trying to take up all the room in the frame. This cracks everyone up, which is manna for my soul. (I am known, in some circles, as someone who will do just about anything for a laugh.)

As more and more people try to squeeze into the photos, the crowd becomes increasingly boisterous and giddy. This is an experience I've had in other parts of the world, including the Middle East and South America, where the excitement of capturing a particular, and perhaps rare, kind of human connection becomes too much to contain.

Once the tiny, delighted crowd disperses, we are free to explore the other structures and courtyards that inhabit the City Palace, each with its own title and history. Our photo shoot took place in front of the Mubarak Mahal, a museum whose name means Auspicious Palace and that displays silk-embroidered royal attire, such as hats, coats, capes, and shoes.

After admiring the intricate stitchery and tie-dyed silks, everyone is eager for the Pritam Niwas Chowk, or Peacock Courtyard. Here we can admire its four famed doorways, each of which was designed to represent different Hindu gods and the four seasons. Each doorway sits in a recessed entryway with scalloped edges that make me feel like I'm standing below a giant seashell.

It is in the Peacock Courtyard where I see, in vivid detail, much of the inspiration for Vineeta's artwork. Her artwork is displayed on an array of home and kitchen accessories, such as mugs, trays, boxes, ceramics, and coasters, and she incorporates into her work many of the same images, patterns, and palettes I see at City Palace: peacock motifs, lotus flowers, roses, and turban-clad figures composed in fuschia, moss green, gold, and royal blue.

In all my years as an artist, and with a wide circle of artist friends, this is an experience I have never had—one where I am able to literally stand in the middle of the artist's muse and see it, plain as day. I can imagine and comprehend other artists' inspirations. I am able, on a purely rational level, to create something of a map in my mind that places artists I know alongside likely influences, interests, and passions, and my idea of this might land in the general vicinity of where they would place themselves. But with Vineeta's work, I get to stand smack in the middle of it.

After taking our own bunch of goofy selfies beneath the arch of the southwest lotus gate, we go for lunch at a restaurant chosen by Vineeta and Nisha. From there we visit Anokhi, a spacious, light-filled boutique that offers block-printed textiles—clothing, table linens, journals, and other handmade items—all of which are offered at unfathomably low price points.

We return to our hotel in the early evening. Barb, Jennette, and I still feel less than entirely healthy, so we've decided it's prudent to end the day early and save our energy for the next morning's visit to the Amber Fort.

After hugging Vineeta and Nisha good night, the four of us decide to drop our bags in our rooms and reconvene at our hotel's poolside bar for a nightcap. While seated at a table beneath the scalloped archways that surround the bar, we admire the turquoise and navy blue honeycomb pattern on the pool's surface and the bright crescent moon that hangs in the sky like a lantern. We receive our drinks and a few small snacks and contemplate our last hours in India. Tomorrow we will be in Agra, where we'll stay one night, and the night after that we'll spend a few hours in a hotel in Delhi before our 2:00 a.m. flights back to the United States.

The clock is ticking down to the one-year anniversary of the death of Barb's mom, which is tomorrow. Her mom has maintained a strong presence throughout our trip. Barb felt her watching over all of us, Kolleen in particular, on our bicycle ride through Delhi. On our second evening in Varanasi, when Barb and I went to the Ganga Aarti on our own while Jennette and Kolleen tucked into bed early, she shared with me her worries about whether or not she had done enough for her mom during the last weeks she was alive. This was when Barb was by her side almost twenty-four hours a day. My initial response was to say, "Of course you did!" Thankfully, I quickly understood she wasn't sharing this in order to receive a pat on the back or some kind of assurance that she'd done the best she could. She didn't need anything that night except for me to be quiet and listen while the ceremonial bells rang, the priests tossed marigolds in the air, and the smoke from Varanasi's main cremation area churned into the sky downriver.

Tonight I make a toast to Barb's mom, honoring her for raising such an extraordinary daughter. Before I've finished, Barb begins to sob. After her tears stop flowing, she shares something she has learned from the death of her mom.

"It doesn't matter if your relationship is close, nonexistent, or troubled," she begins, "but when your mom dies, you immediately wonder how you're ever going to be able to do *anything* again."

In the middle of Jaipur, on our second-to-last full night in India, Barb has laid down a profound truth Kolleen, Jennette, and I have yet to fully appreciate. It is an insight I know will stay with me and become a permanent reminder that the time I now have with my own mom, who is in her early seventies and healthy, is not to be squandered. That Barb has shared it with us in such stark yet compassionate terms is an act of generosity I know I can't yet fathom.

The sky is dark but clear, the temperature perfect. The four of us sit quietly, absorbing Barb's words. The muffle of distant voices on the far side of the pool, where the restaurant is, wafts toward us like dandelion seeds. I hear the faint sound of silverware clinking on china and the sound of ice settling in my glass as it melts. There is nowhere on earth I'd rather be and no other company I'd rather have.

After saying good night, we retreat to our rooms to prepare for tomorrow's journey. As I wash my face, brush my teeth, and organize a few final items in my suitcase, I am thinking about the pace of our trip. It went from full speed ahead in Delhi and Varanasi, came to a complete stop in Samode, and has only gradually picked up momentum since. While I was ready to experience everything I possibly could during our first week here, my determination to take in as much as humanly possible waned once we reached Samode, where most of us were sick and exhausted.

Our travel agent had provided us with a carefully curated list of options for our time in Jaipur based on our interests, and now that our only full day here is over, I'm aware we've experienced just a fraction of them. On our way into the city, we missed scheduled visits to a handmade paper studio and a textile house. We didn't see the Govind Dev Ji Temple. We won't get anywhere near the Jantar Mantar, the world's largest stone observatory.

So much time was spent planning and coordinating all of this—and we had to travel halfway around the world to be here—that it is tempting to feel guilty about the way many of the arrangements have been, in the end, dismissed. But the guilt evaporates quickly in the face of other priorities, such as my health and my friends. I was content turning away from opportunities to see and do more in Jaipur because it meant I could attend to those concerns. With fewer items on the schedule, I could conserve energy and give my body more time to recover from being sick. In the process, I was given the gift of more time to truly *be* with my friends.

It isn't easy to travel with another person, let alone three, let alone *in India*. With our ambitious itinerary and our particular bundle of difficulties, it has taken no small measure of patience, self-possession, and kindness for us to maintain balance and calm. Each of us has had to attend to our own self-care and, in turn, fully honor whatever that needed to look like for anyone else. We've had to coordinate when to meet for meals, decide how much time to spend at various places, and keep track of shared expenses. We've had to allow for—and, when possible, help allay—fears and concerns that arose along the way. Knowing my twice-sprained ankles can be wobbly on a good day, all three of my travel mates made a committed effort to warn me about potholes, steps, and uneven pavement everywhere we went. We've shared our tissues, cold pills, energy bars, and ginger candies. We've helped each other squeeze through the tight spots that threatened to overwhelm us. We've laughed so hard our stomachs hurt when we found those situations comical. And we've chosen, moment by moment, to be kind, patient, accepting, compassionate.

That we have made it this far not merely tolerating each other but loving each other more deeply than ever is a testament to the courage and graciousness of these women.

When wading through circumstances that place me squarely outside what's familiar, priorities become crystal clear, creating a razor-sharp outline of what's most important. I have been well acquainted with this experience during this past year of moving across country. With a long list of friends and family left behind in Southern California, I've had to consider: How will I maintain close connections with them from the Midwest? Is that even possible? Now that I will need to get on an airplane to see people who used to live in my neighborhood, how will that affect other relationships that have always been long distance?

I have come to consider the last twelve months as The Year of Heartbreaking Choices. As soon as we began seriously exploring the possibility of moving, decisions I would normally have breezed through became exercises in staying fiercely focused on my most important values. This started with the move itself, which was a decision I would likely never have initiated and had a millions reasons to *not* want to do, were it not for my husband's deep unhappiness. It could not be ignored, and it paved the way for a detour I never saw coming but consciously chose to embrace.

Because of our move, I chose not to teach a workshop with a dear friend in Northern California. I wasn't able to attend the graduation party of the daughter of my best friend in high school, a young woman I've known since she was a baby. I missed the summer solstice parade in Santa Barbara, my favorite day of the year. Time after time, it was necessary for me to zero in on what mattered most in situations where multiple options were meaningful in their own way.

I can't say my decision to devote my time and energy to my friends instead of the items on our travel agent's "Highlights of Jaipur" list is a terribly devastating one, but it falls in the realm of circumstances that don't allow me to run through the candy store and grab everything in sight. Today I didn't see much of Jaipur, but I got to spend hours talking to my friends. Tonight I'll be heading to bed early. By conserving energy, I'll decrease the chance of waking up tomorrow feeling worn out and less able to enjoy my last morning with Vineeta and Nisha. These haven't been hard choices, but they've been calculated. By clarifying what's most important, the answers to my questions rise up like a bud through the ground, beckoning me forward on the most meaningful path possible.

JANUARY 22, 2018 *Jagat Shiromani*

I'm beginning to organize my belongings for the last leg of our trip. This is one of my travel quirks—to reorganize my suitcases at each stop—and it's a habit Barb found comical on our first trip to India. While I brought one large suitcase, a carry-on case, and an empty duffel bag in 2014, all of which were stuffed full by the time Barb and I headed home, I only carried one medium-sized suitcase and a backpack this time, which has forced me to make more methodical and precise purchases. More than anything, my treasures from India are flat, small, and lightweight, consisting mainly of vintage textiles, small antique figures, and a few bottles of essential oils from Varanasi.

This morning we will meet up with Vineeta and Nisha so we can visit the Amber Fort and the Jagat Shiromani Temple, dedicated to Krishna and Vishnu, before saying goodbye and then driving to Agra for the Taj Mahal. And so I am packing and organizing everything for the journey home, setting aside clothing for my last full day in India plus the flight home so it is easily retrievable from my suitcase.

It is hard to believe our trip is coming to an end. The time has not been what I thought it would be, and it has been more than I could have ever asked for. I don't know whether I am braver than I realized or more of a delicate flower. Perhaps both, one bolstered and made meaningful by the other.

I didn't come to India without fear or trepidation; I came despite those things. My equilibrium got knocked loose far earlier into the trip than I'd anticipated (I knew it would happen eventually), but I also managed to find a place of deep, internal stillness in almost every situation. I learned the value of a long, deep breath and sank into my practice of turning to God in times of both need and gratitude. I never gave up on my friends, and they never gave up on me. Even with all of India's disconcerting elements, I'm still in love with her.

The weather is warm and sunny, and our visit to the Amber Fort—a vast complex of sandstone and marble courtyards and structures situated on a hill not far outside Jaipur's city limits—is fun. We ogle the intricate tile work of the Sheesh Mahal, or Mirror Palace, and are entertained by a troop of monkeys leaping and dangling above our heads. Although the complex is massive, it is crowded with tourists, many of whom are wearing the cheap souvenir turbans being sold in the main courtyard. We wind our way up, down, and through a network of stairs, hallways, and small alcoves that provide expansive views of the Amber Fort Wall, the third largest wall in the world.

Afterward, we are taken to the Jagat Shiromani Temple in a covered Jeep. We remain quiet during the drive, watching a steady procession of elephants pass us on the road. Elephant rides to the Amber Fort are a popular tourist activity, something that makes all four of us bristle. The elephants we see appear to be done for the day, heading back to wherever they are kept until they return to the fort for their next shift. My camera remains tucked inside my bag, as the idea of photographing the elephants feels invasive and exploitative. They are not in their natural habitat; they aren't walking past us on a narrow city street of their own volition.

We are, all six of us, absorbed in our own thoughts. After our next stop, our time together will come to an end, and then Jennette, Kolleen, Barb, and I will proceed to Agra for our last night's sleep in India. The mood is relaxed but contemplative. Our heads sway from side to side as the vehicle maneuvers up hills, between parked cars, and past the crowds.

The Jagat Shiromani Temple, constructed in the early 1600s, is relatively small and sits atop a set of stairs flanked by two smooth, marble elephant statues as tall as I am. A woman in an emerald green sari makes an offering at a small shrine in the main courtyard. A camel-colored dog sprawls in the sunlight. Inside the temple, a pigeon sits serenely atop the head of a relief sculpture of Krishna. I notice an old, battered piece of stereo equipment covered in dust and cobwebs sitting inside a rectangular niche of the temple wall. A blinding fluorescent tube light, the kind seen in gas station bathrooms, hangs above the temple's entrance, and it shows off tiny relief sculptures of elephants, horses, trees, and human figures holding umbrellas, bows and arrows, and even snakes above the entryway.

As I face the temple's main worship area, a man deposits an offering of oranges and a few rupees. To my left I see a sunny alcove with a perfectly made bed—or, really, what looks to be a long table with a thin mattress and bedspread on it. A clean, white, collared shirt hangs in one of the windowsills. The area is tidy and bright, with a few humble signs of modernity, such as the pale yellow bed cover that practically glows in contrast to the muted rust and ivory hues of the temple. The space of the area is small—no bigger than a walk-in closet—and it has been perfectly swept. It is a place for the *pandit*, or Hindu priest, to rest when he is not ministering to worshippers.

I love the grand palaces, with their turquoise, garnet, and lapis embellished tilework, marble latticework, and symmetrically designed gardens, but these smaller spaces command my attention and pull it in specific, more intimate directions. I've zoomed in on and been awed by the smaller details in the City Palace and Amber Fort, but the scale of this temple encourages deeper breaths and more sustained stillnesses. There is only so much to look at, only so much area to cover.

Knowing I will be in the presence of the grandest of all of India's monuments—the Taj Mahal—in less than twenty-four hours, I savor my time in this lesser-known sacred space. I listen to the chants of the temple's holy man as he ministers to the worshippers, and I hear the pigeon flap its wings. There are no crowds of tourists or vendors hawking souvenirs. It is only me, my friends, and the locals attending to their faith. Just outside, the world spins madly on, and the elephants go home to rest.

JANUARY 22, 2018 *I Want to Know*

We've just dropped off Vineeta and Nisha and said our goodbyes. I am a weepy, blubbery mess, and I use up yet another packet of tissues. Everyone has settled quietly into their seats for the three-hour drive to Agra. No one tries to comfort me or tells me it's okay. I am grateful for this—for my friends' ability and willingness to simply hold the space for my sadness, just as we did last night for Barb.

I think about what a remarkable exploit it is that all four of us have managed to do the most important thing we could do on this trip, which is to let India be India. In the same way, we have allowed each other to be whatever and wherever we've needed to be emotionally, physically, and spiritually. We have all shed tears; we have all prayed. We have all chosen rest over an excursion. We have all talked of how eager we are to bring some of India's mystery and beauty back home with us. We have all experienced a chasm opening in our hearts, whereupon a glittering trove of jewels spilled out like an unopened gift we never knew was waiting for us. I have observed something in each of my friends that I might have known was always there but never saw expressed with such vigor—Kolleen's joy, Jennette's vulnerability, Barb's steadfastness.

What I want right now more than anything is to know when and how I will see Vineeta and Nisha again. I feel the passage of time, and I ponder the fact that our visits have been three and four years apart, respectively. If that is a realistic amount of time to pass before we can connect in person again, I wonder how many more opportunities I will have to share a meal with them. I am grateful, profoundly grateful, for what we've had—and I also want to know. I want to know this won't be our last goodbye.

What I understand, instead, is this: It is not possible for me to know with total certainty when or how or even if I will see Vineeta and Nisha again. This is true about everyone and everything. I do an astounding job of deluding myself into thinking I know the when, where, and how of time with my friends, of my work, and even for running errands. And while much of the time things do unfold in the way I arrange, there is always—*always*—the possibility that some unforeseen and perhaps even dreaded force will sweep in and wreak havoc on my perfectly outlined plans. Is this the hardest truth for me, for most of us, to embrace—that we are ultimately not in control?

I want to know my husband and I will grow old together. I want to know I will be able to write for as many years as I am inspired to write. I want to know we are all going to make it home safely. The list of things I want to know will and won't happen is endless, even though I also know pondering it is futile. This dichotomy is at the source of the mystery of life, that ephemeral space where all that is unknown makes everything in the here and now so precious. The fleeting nature of every moment and all that these experiences hold is the precise encouragement that has me so deeply committed to *presence*. In every moment I have in this wild and crazy world, I want to be exactly where I am and nowhere else. I want to live in full acceptance of all that I don't know and, in that act of surrender, to sink into what I have, wherever I happen to be.

Right now, where I happen to be is in a van, a pile of wadded-up tissues in my lap, eyes red from crying. It is just about forty hours before I am supposed to go home. It is sitting in a vehicle with three of the dearest people I know on earth. It is a moment that has me missing my husband and wondering when I will be back in Santa Barbara. It is, like every other minute of my existence, its own tiny universe—full of sparkle and wonder and an ephemeral yet enduring, unbridled joy.

LAKSHMI

Lakshmi is the Hindu goddess of wealth, fortune, and prosperity. Lakshmi in Sanskrit is derived from the root word Laks, meaning to perceive, observe, know, and understand.

As our bus creeps toward our hotel in Agra, the last place we will rest our heads in India, we are surrounded. Tour buses, cars, and other automobiles press in around us, full of what I assume are other tour groups. It has only been four years since my last visit, but from the looks of this evening's traffic, Agra's popularity has exploded.

Our collective energy has become quiet and tense. Right in the middle of lunch, the mood took a sharp left turn when Jennette started to get sick again. Within a couple of hours, when we stopped to visit Fatehpur Sikri—a former Mughal capital built in the sixteenth century—on the outskirts of Agra, Jennette was back to being miserable, unable to take the short tour through the monument. With all the unexpected congestion in Agra, I start to dread the possibility that we will see the Taj Mahal with a mob of tourists and without Jennette.

It takes some time to get checked into our rooms. The crowd at our hotel is different from anywhere else we've been. I don't get the impression we'll run into any nice British women offering over-the-counter cold and flu medication like we did in Samode. Instead, we are repeatedly interrupted by two women insistent on having their questions answered by the hotel clerk who is trying to take care of us. Larger groups of people stream in and out of the hotel; cliques of four or more move boisterously through the lobby. My only desire in this moment is to find our room, go inside, and stay there until the next morning.

We arrange for one of our two rooms to be given a cot so Jennette can have a room to herself. Her energy has deteriorated quickly, and she cannot be far from a bathroom. Although we don't say it, I understand that as we watch our friend wither before our eyes, all four of us have our impending departure in mind. What if another one of us gets this sick? Will Jennette be able to fly home? If not, what happens then?

The one night three of us need to share a room, we happen to be in the smallest hotel room of the entire trip. But we don't mind. It turns out everyone has the same idea I do, and we agree we are in for the night. We get Jennette settled in her room and then return to ours, eager to prepare ourselves for the final stretch, which includes the Taj Mahal, followed by the four-hour drive to Delhi, where we will have time to get ourselves ready for our flights home.

Barb, Kolleen, and I order room service. Our order includes french fries. When they arrive, they are the best french fries I've ever had in my life.

Ever since I got sick here, I have subsisted on the same basic meals for breakfast, lunch, and dinner. In the morning, it's been a cheese omelet, *roti*, and, if available, fresh pineapple. To top it off, I usually can't resist the sweeter offerings on most breakfast buffets—small chocolate donuts, in particular. For lunch and dinner, I've relied on *dal makhani*, butter *naan*, vegetable *biryani*, and the occasional bowl of mulligatawny soup. By Indian standards, these aren't bland meals (nothing is bland in India), but they are mild enough to allow me to eat to my heart's content. Turns out, traveling around India while battling a sinus infection makes me ravenous. Back at home, when I'm not feeling well, I turn to chicken pot pies and toaster waffles. In India, it's this.

My overall approach to dining in India started with trusting our travel agent. On both trips, tour guides have offered precise food-related directives. At one small eatery full of locals in the Chandni Chowk market in 2014, our tour guide ordered for Barb and me and pointed out what we could and could not eat in the condiment trays. As this was our first full day in India, it immediately put me on notice that our travel agent had fully vetted every café, restaurant, and roadside eatery, ensuring they could accommodate our Western constitutions. I also avoid meat in India, not only to reduce the risk of food poisoning, but also because it feels strange to eat meat in a country where vegetarianism is the norm.

Beyond that, I don't spend a lot of time trying to analyze every menu option available. I go with what sounds good, which, on this trip, happens to be pretty much the same thing at every meal. I also manage the spice levels when I order, which can be adjusted in most dishes as long as I specify "not too spicy." (*Hot* does not equal *spicy*; *hot* only refers to temperature.)

Between our travel agent, our tour guides, hotel restaurants, and the encouragement of Vineeta and Nisha, I have been able to enjoy a banquet's worth of delectable dishes. I've wiped clean plates of *dals*, curries, chutneys, and *paranthas*. But if I had to pick a favorite dish, it would be the Rajasthani *thali*, which consists of six to eight dishes served in small metal cups arranged on a large platter with rice, a few accompaniments, and a generous serving of *roti* on the side. The cups hold lentils, chickpeas, green beans, cauliflower, and potatoes prepared with tomatoes, garlic, ginger, turmeric, mustard seeds, chili powder, and *garam masala*. The traditional way of eating it is without utensils, using one's fingers and the *roti* to scoop up helpings of each dish in lieu of a fork or spoon. It was with the *thali* that Barb and I learned the importance of the after-dinner finger bowls. Once our dishes were cleared, a small bowl with a lemon wedge was set before us, an invitation to wash our hands.

Tonight, though, I am deliriously happy with the plate of french fries perched in the middle of our bed. With every bite, I happily groan, grateful for the wonders of potatoes fried in oil.

VEGETABLE BIRYANI

SPICED YOGURT SAUCE

1 ¼ cup plain yogurt
3/4 tsp ground cumin
3/4 tsp ground coriander
3/4 tsp ground cinnamon
Pinch of cayenne pepper
¼ tsp salt

Mix everything together
in a small bowl. Keep
chilled until ready to
serve biryani.

(serves 4)

2 T ghee*
1 small onion, diced
1 small bell pepper, diced
2 tsp garam masala
1 tsp ground cumin
1 tsp ground coriander
½ tsp ground cardamon
½ tsp turmeric powder
½ tsp chile powder
1 bay leaf
1 cup peas (fresh or frozen)
1 cup chopped green beans
2 medium carrots, chopped into matchsticks
1 cup Indian basmati rice
2 cups vegetable broth or water
3/4 tsp salt
Small handful chopped mint
Small handful chopped cilantro (optional)
½ cup cashews, lightly toasted
1/3 cup raisins

* or neutral cooking oil

In medium Dutch oven (or other heavy-bottomed
pot), heat the oil over medium-high heat. Sauté
the onion and bell pepper until soft, about
4-5 minutes. Stir in all the spices and cook
until fragrant, about 1-2 minutes.

Add the remaining peas, green beans, and
carrots, and stir well. Add the broth and
salt. Adjust heat to high and cook until
boiling. Cover the pot and reduce heat to low.
Cook for 20 minutes, or until rice is soft.
Keep the biryani covered and let it rest 5
minutes away from the heat. Use a large fork
to fluff the rice as you mix in the chopped
mint and cilantro, as well as the cashews and
raisins. Serve immediately, accompanied by
spiced yogurt sauce.

DAL MAKHANI

(serves 4-6)

1 cup urad dal or black "beluga" lentils,
  soaked overnight and drained
2/3 cup adzuki beans, soaked overnight
  and drained
2 T ghee or neutral cooking oil
1 onion, diced
3 cloves garlic, minced
1-inch piece of ginger, peeled and
  finely grated
1 T garam masala
1 tsp ground cumin
1 tsp ground coriander
1 tsp chile powder
½ tsp ground cardamom
½ tsp turmeric powder
1 cinnamon stick
1 bay leaf
1 14.5-ounce can diced tomatoes
3 T tomato paste
½ cup heavy cream or full-fat coconut milk
1 tsp salt

Place lentils and adzuki beans in a medium pot
and cover with water by 1 inch. Bring to a boil
over high heat, and then reduce heat to medium-
low and cover the pot. Cook for 30-35 minutes,
until tender. Drain and rinse with cool water.
(This step can be done ahead of time and cooked
lentils/beans can be stored in the refrigerator
until ready to use.)

In a medium Dutch oven or other heavy-bottomed
pot, heat the ghee/oil over medium-high heat.
Add the onion and cook for 7-8 minutes, or until
translucent. Stir in the garlic and ginger and
cook for 1 minute more. Add the spices, as well
as the tomatoes (and their juices) and the
tomato paste. Stir well.

Stir in the cooked lentils/beans and add 1½ cups
of water. Once the dal begins to bubble, reduce
heat to low and cook uncovered for 30-35
minutes, stirring occasionally, until sauce
is noticeably thicker. Stir in the heavy cream
or coconut milk, as well as the salt. Allow dal
to cook for an additional 10-15 minutes. Taste
dal and add more spices (chile powder or garam
masala) or salt, as desired. Serve dal immediately,
or keep it covered over a very low flame until
ready to serve.

JANUARY 22, 2018 *Prayers, Again*

In addition to the french fries, Barb has ordered a bottle of champagne in honor of her mom, Karen, who passed away one year ago today. This has been on my mind since this morning, and I have kept a close eye on Barb all day. As we got settled in our room, unzipping suitcases and setting out toiletries, she pulled us together for a prayer. We faced each other, held hands, bowed our heads, and offered up prayers of gratitude for Karen's life, for her daughter, and for all the ways she watched over us during our time in India.

As we prayed, my mind wandered back to our time in Varanasi, where all four of us felt our hearts crack open. At one point I overheard Barb talking to our guide, Dinesh, about being with her mom during the last weeks of her life and the moment she passed away. Barb said, "As soon as my mom died, I suddenly felt her *everywhere* and felt her love for me expand to *everything*. It was a gift I could only receive *after* she died." It was the same experience I had with my grandma. Without the physical limitations of her body, there were no limits to where her presence could be felt. What was for eighty-five years condensed and contained within a vessel of bones, organs, and blood vessels could take flight, expand, and disperse—even to India.

My friends and I are at that stage in life—the one where we must come to terms not only with the passing of the people who raised us, but also with the ensuing generational rearrangement that puts us squarely in the category of Next in Line. After Barb's mom died a year ago, another friend's father succumbed to cancer. Within four months of my return from India, I will watch one of my oldest and dearest friends mourn the unexpected deterioration and passing of her dad.

I have many friends whose parents are still active and healthy, and this is true for me as well, but I still feel like I am walking along a tightrope. On one end is where my parents', and my own, demise can be seen as a faint mirage in the distance, something I know is there, but it shimmers, shapeshifts, and sometimes vanishes; I can block it out of my mind without too much effort. On the other end is where I am officially an orphan, parents gone and buried and no one left to take the leap into the ultimate unknown except me. I know if I end up making it that far—watching my parents leave, growing into an old woman—I'll be one of the lucky ones.

I'm not sure I see any rhyme or reason to the timing and method of our being plucked out of this existence. Why did my husband's mom have to die when he was a baby? Why did my best friend's brother have to die just before he finished high school? What was the grand plan behind the death of my friend Linda, who lost her battle with cancer mere weeks after her fiftieth birthday? Death tends to inspire more questions than answers, even if I am open to all the ways a soul can exist, both in and beyond our human form.

I like to think that should my husband depart before me, I will be able to maintain and be comforted by a deep well of gratitude for the time I had with him, but I don't bother trying to prepare myself in this way or any other. Grief has brought me to my knees at different times of my life, and the thought of what she might have in store for me if I lose the love of my life is, if I'm honest with myself, terrifying. I don't want to know what it is to live without him. But in marrying him, I've agreed to take that risk. This is a fundamental element of loving deeply, whether as a parent, a child, a lover, a friend, or a dog owner. As soon as we agree to love with all of our hearts, we agree to endure the grief that will most assuredly sweep in should the object of our love be taken away.

In love, there exists a strange, precarious, unsettling sweet spot, where the temptation to guard against the worst of grief's storm can loom large. But just like my time in Jaipur taught me, love can encourage a clear and determined reckoning with my values. While there, I asked myself what was more important—seeing buildings or my friends?

Risking exhaustion or getting rest? In my marriage, I go through the same routine, asking myself what means more—avoiding intimacy or encouraging it? Running away from potential future pain or letting in as much joy as possible right now? I am confronted with this choice in all kinds of situations, including the ones that call upon me to work through my heart's worst tangles and question my own assumptions. Sometimes it is my vulnerability that creates greater intimacy, and other times what is needed is a determination to stand confidently in my marriage—to trust that whatever storms we have to endure together will only strengthen our bond.

The idea of expending energy trying *not* to love, to somehow manage its unpredictable currents, seems such a mammoth waste of time, which is another lesson of India—the way it implores me to be disciplined and exacting in where and how I direct my efforts. Moments wasted on trying to resist what is can never be retrieved.

Here on earth, I can watch a caterpillar curl into itself and disappear into a shroud of its own making. In this realm, I am able to see the result of its permutation and the moment it sheds its old form in order to embark upon an entirely new existence. One of the most earthbound creatures in the world, with a body that clings to and stretches across the ground (or stem or leaf) to get where it needs to go, will now move through the world on wings, free to flutter across forests, rivers, and even state lines.

I, too, will go through such a metamorphosis. The difference is that when I retreat into the abyss and then release myself from the body that carried me through whatever years I will have been blessed to receive, no one will see my spirit emerge in its new form. (Or maybe someone will—who's to say?)

I do not believe for a moment that my soul will disintegrate along with my body. I do not believe my grandma or Barb's mom are wholly *gone*. Barb's mom is always with her. I know this because Barb says so, and I believe her. She was with us during our bicycle ride through Delhi, on the days we got sick, and during the train ride around Deogarh. My grandma appeared in the face of a woman in Varanasi, just as she shows up in the birdsong I hear outside my window back at home. I look at my hands and see hers. I pull weeds in my garden and feel her right alongside me.

One of the ways I express love back home has me praying quietly on my meditation cushion now. These prayers don't come from anything that can be seen; they never go anywhere that can be recorded. But it is my hope that, in the end, these prayers will be delivered, perhaps in the form of a psychic telegram, to everyone I've ever prayed for. As they emerge into a new way of being and get ready to spread their wings, maybe my words will swoop beneath them, lifting them up to the heavens:

> *You were always deeply loved.*
> *You will be forever.*
> *Eternally yours, Christine*

In honor of love and all the ways it manages to poke holes through the universe, the three of us raise our glasses—a toast to a woman named Karen, a woman I've never met but whom I love just the same.

In all my travels, I have enjoyed seeing some of the more well-known wonders of the world and have been surprisingly awed by just a few—Argentina's Iguazu Falls and the Pacific Coast Highway through Big Sur, California, come to mind as two places whose hype dramatically undersold the actual experience. I have also been overcome with emotion upon the fulfillment a long-held dream, such as seeing Petra in Jordan.

I am not immune to the charms of the world's most notorious wonders. People are drawn to and fascinated by the Eiffel Tower, the Great Barrier Reef, the Terracotta Warriors, and the giant Redwoods because they wake something up in us. Through art and architecture, I haven't merely learned about history; I've also witnessed the kind of creativity that has been brought to life through a seemingly direct channel to God. In nature, I've gotten a glimpse of the intelligence behind the order and design of the cosmos, recognizing the mysterious yet precise structure and beauty of this planet.

Despite all of this, nothing prepared me for my first glimpse of the famed white marble mausoleum on the banks of the Yamuna River—the Taj Mahal. Barb and I came perilously close to moving right past what the locals refer to as "the Taj" on our 2014 trip, believing it couldn't possibly be as awe-inspiring as everyone said. When Kolleen and Jennette expressed the same initial ambivalence, Barb and I insisted we put it on our route.

"Trust us," we said. "You will be so happy we went."

We crawled out of bed while it was still dark for this sunrise visit to the Taj Mahal. My excitement at getting to see it again has been doused and made soggy by the tenacity of Jennette's illness—that she won't be going with us is a monumental disappointment, no pun intended. Knowing

Jennette is miserable and alone in our hotel is a fact of this last full day in India I am sure I won't ever release. And after seeing the hordes of giant tour buses as we arrived in Agra yesterday evening, I wonder if today's outing is going to end up being the most anticlimactic part of our trip.

But the line of visitors waiting to get in as soon as the monument opens is not long at all. This was true four years ago, as well, when Barb and I were here at the same time with the same tour guide, Tarun. On that first visit, we miraculously managed to be the very first people to enter, which gave us a precious few moments with the Taj entirely to ourselves. Even Tarun was ecstatic. "I've been a guide here for fifteen years," he explained, "and this has *never* happened."

Men and women enter through different pathways and are frisked on their way in. When the woman in charge of patting me down discovers a cough drop in my pocket, she makes me dispose of it. I wince the moment I release it onto a tiny pile of other such contraband. This is the last of my honey lemon Ricola drops, which have soothed a throat run ragged by coughing fits. I get it—the Taj Mahal is no place to risk having candy or gum disposed of and stuck—but I want to plead with the woman not to deprive me of this tiny creature comfort. Instead, I keep moving, aware this is a small disappointment compared to what lies beyond the main archway ahead of me.

A few minutes later, we are in. We are not the only ones here, but the crowd is small. (Never underestimate the allure of sleeping in.)

When the Taj Mahal comes into view, it doesn't look like something built as much as something that crystallized into existence, molecule by molecule. It isn't until I stand close enough to touch it that I am convinced it is constructed with an undeniably solid material: marble.

Commissioned in 1632 by Shah Jahan, a Mughal emperor, this mausoleum holds the tomb of his wife, Mumtaz Mahal, and is, for lack of a better word, perfect. Entering the grounds of the Taj, I can't help but feel as if I've stepped into a dream state; I wouldn't be surprised to see a unicorn strolling in the grass. The composition of the entire forty-two-acre property, which includes the Taj Mahal, the reflecting pool, a mosque, the gardens, and other outlying buildings, evinces a sense of order and design that feels almost otherworldly in its precision. I wonder if this is the reason I have such a visceral response to it—its attention to geometric and algorithmic balance. Patterns we find in everything, from the spiral of sunflower seeds to seashells, from honeycombs to snowflakes, follow rules of mathematical order that can be described as nothing less than musical. From such compositions, something beautiful emerges. This is the same wonderment I experience when I stand within the universe of the Taj.

Most visitors to this monument are moved by the fact that it came into existence because of an emperor's love for his wife. While this is a poignant story, I feel my pulse quicken at the thought of all the minds and hands that worked together to bring this vision to life. Out of nothing came this. The mere spark of an idea—and the love of one man for his wife—brought into being something that draws seven to eight million visitors each year and as many as seventy thousand per day. Some travel here for the love story; others for its history. Whatever the motivation, no one sees the Taj and goes home unmoved. This is why everyone I knew who'd been there told me I *had* to go.

The three of us make our way forward, and I once again reflect on the differences between my experience today versus four years ago. Barb and I walked these grounds at the beginning of our trip in 2014, when we were still acclimating to the clamor and energy of India. We were wide-eyed and giddy, with most of our adventures still ahead of us. We hadn't fully emerged from the state of disbelief that we were in *India*. Even though I know our sunrise visit that day was shrouded in the same chilly fog that surrounds us this morning, my memory of it is awash in sunlight.

Today I am here under a different set of circumstances and with different things on my mind—namely, that I'll be on my way home in less than twenty-four hours, unless Jennette's illness necessitates an adjustment to those plans. I have, since yesterday, kept a space in my mind free from any concern beyond the one I have for her journey home. I take in the dreamy vision of the most famous mausoleum in the world, and I send up a prayerful vision of Jennette, and all of us, getting back to our homes and families safe, sound, and without any last-minute changes to flight schedules. At the same time, I prepare myself for the possibility that revisions might have to happen. There has been no discussion about this, and I'm not *worried* about it, but I consider the gentle loosening of my grip on my plans to be prudent and measured.

As I approach the domed mausoleum and admire the same garnet, lapis, and turquoise inlays I gushed over four years ago, I think about all that has transpired—in India, in the world, in my life—since I was last here. I wonder if I'll ever be here again, and if I'll ever be back in India. I don't ask these questions because my love for India has waned but because, well, how am I to know? What does life have in store for me in the coming year, or even next week? When I was here four years ago, moving to Wisconsin wasn't even a whisper of an idea. Yet here I am, with a return plane ticket taking me to O'Hare.

I've visited plenty of places I've sworn I would return to someday, only to have other circumstances keep me away. The flip side of this is that other parts of the world have pulled me toward them in unexpected ways. Many of my most meaningful journeys have happened through chance encounters, random conversations, or the dew drop of an idea that quickly transformed into a cascade of travel arrangements. If I am meant to return to India after this trip, then I will be back. If I'm not, then perhaps I'll be directed somewhere else. Either way, there's only one thing for me to do right now: be fully present to this time, this place, this miracle.

THE TAJ MAHAL

Commissioned in 1632 by the Mughal emperor
Shah Jahan to house the tomb of his favorite
wife, Mumtaz Mahal

Date completed: 1653

Architectural Style: Mughal

20,000+: Number of artisans who
worked on and built the Taj Mahal

1000: Number of elephants that
helped transport building materials

8 million: Number of annual visitors

240 feet: Height of Taj Mahal

Taj Mahal is one of the Seven
Wonders of the World and a
UNESCO World Heritage Site.

Cars and buses are prohibited
from coming within 500 meters
(1040 feet) of the Taj Mahal.

Calligraphy of
Persian poems and
passages of the
Quran were used as
decorative elements
all over the
complex.

The four 130-foot tall minarets
on each corner of the platform
supporting the Taj Mahal were
intentionally built to lean
slightly outward so that if any
of them fall, they would fall
away from the Taj Mahal.

More than twenty
types of precious
and semi-precious
stones were used
to adorn Taj Mahal,
including agate,
lapis, turquoise,
ruby, coral, jade,
and malachite.

EPILOGUE

I have boarded my flight and am settled in for the long journey home. The four of us said our farewells in the main terminal a few hours ago, each of us heading in different directions. Barb and Kolleen will travel home on the same flight, but Jennette and I are each on our own.

Releasing Jennette into the wilds of international air travel by herself while she was feeling so miserable and sick—literally on death's door, as she would later describe it—was one of the biggest exercises in trust I've ever endured. I've sent text messages to everyone I can think of back home, requesting focused, concentrated prayers for her safe journey. Barb told her to dig deep; Kolleen hugged her tight; I looked her in the eyes and told her to take every step of the process she was about to begin one at a time. As I sit here waiting for my plane to pull back from the gate, I continue the litany of prayers I've been keeping up since yesterday. *Please get Jennette home safely. Please let her rest on the flights.*

She does, in fact, get home without much incident. After being grilled by the captain of her Lufthansa flight on the nature of her illness and symptoms, she is allowed to board and have all of her bags checked for free. I won't know this for almost twenty-four hours, but I am well acquainted with the strength of my friend's will and determination. In that, I renew my confidence in her ability to make it across the Atlantic and all the way to Seattle.

As I settle into my seat, I do so with the awareness that much of my life back home is mundane. I spend far more time scrubbing dishes than I do wandering foreign lands, and I have washed hundreds of loads of laundry. One of my daily tasks is picking up my dog's poop.

And home, at this particular moment, is still a work in progress. I am not going back to the lush comfort of a place where my loved ones live down the street and I don't need a GPS to run my daily errands. I am going back to a part of the world I can confidently say I'm fond of but don't yet feel I belong. It isn't a place that has held space for me throughout time and eternity, as if it was written in the stars the day the universe exploded into existence that I am meant to be there. *Is Wisconsin where I belong?* I wonder. *Am I going back to the right place? Did I make a monumental mistake transporting myself halfway across the country, or is this going to turn out to be one of the most profound leaps I've ever made?*

The day we pulled out of our driveway to begin the six-day journey east, I felt unmoored, as if I had been let loose in space. In Wisconsin, my husband and I are more geographically isolated, at least from our people, than we've ever been—which hasn't been scary but still feels mysterious. All social and familial ties have been severed and now need to be rewoven. As we figure out those new patterns, we are navigating what it means to be without the comfort and security of an intimate, well-populated nest. We're leaning on each other in ways we've never needed to. We're falling in love in ways we never anticipated.

Once I return from India, when we aren't distracted by the holidays and guests and boxes left to unpack, I know that journey will unfold in a quieter, more contemplative way. There will be snow outside our window, and darkness will come early. The work of reorienting myself to what home means and where it is—or if it even needs to be defined by a specific geographical location—will involve stillness, listening, and, whenever necessary (which might, on some days, be hourly), prayer.

This is the story of my life right now. And God is in all of it, providing me with opportunities for prayer and presence and gratitude *everywhere*, whether I'm walking through the streets of Jaipur, driving on a two-lane highway in Nebraska, or grocery shopping in Milwaukee. If I were to rely on grand moments as the only pathways to enlightenment, I'd miss out on all the wisdom that can be found in the everyday minutiae of adulthood: the wag of my dog's tail, the smell of coffee in my kitchen, a pile of freshly washed towels. My journey might appear to be more holy or spiritually inspired when I'm wandering through the streets of Varanasi, but such travels aren't the only, or even best, way to see God at work in my life and in the world. *Anywhere* I want to see this, I can see it. All I have to do is open my eyes.

To describe India—to catalog the long list of sensory assaults it heaps upon its visitors—is to offer a list nearly as long of reasons to avoid it. All it took was one photo of a bathtub-sized tangle of electrical wires and cables hung precariously above a crowded walkway for my husband to know he never, ever wants to go to India. It is loud and crowded and filled with sights that have the power to stun and sadden and unnerve. When Vineeta, who grew up in the southern state of Kerala, arrived at our hotel in Jaipur in 2014, her first words to me were, "Isn't India *crazy?*" Even the locals aren't immune to its wild temperament.

India moves in a rhythm and flow that is impossible for most Westerners to fathom. It is tempting to look at many facets of India and say they should be "better" or "different" or "fixed." I can hardly claim to know the real India, but I learned a little something of its soul—of the baffling, unfamiliar, and unsettling ways its inhabitants, both human and animal, are provided for. I didn't feel a divine presence in the snapshots of "beauty amidst the squalor"; instead, I felt it in my bones and accepted India as a mysterious jumble of particulars I will never fully understand. The minute I try to attach a label to something—to anything—in India, it is immediately washed over and erased by the tides of the long, complicated story of India.

I return home now knowing only one thing about India with utter certainty, which is that India is . . . well, *India*. It is a world that moves and loves and dances and works in its own spectacular cadence. It is a place where life is hard for most inhabitants but smiles are easy and curiosity is always ready to pounce. It felt daunting and overwhelming and exotic the first time I went, and it feels just as mystifying now. But it is in that bewilderment where India's greatest gifts hide, treasures I will carry home with me in my pocket, talismans for my everyday existence.

As my plane makes its sharp turn onto the runway and I feel the engines rev, I think about the tiger Barb and I saw in Ranthambore four years ago. It is not possible for me to think about India and not recall the tiger. It is as if he is always waiting just beyond the periphery of my awareness, ready to emerge as soon as my thoughts drift to his homeland, the same way he did the day I saw him.

On that morning, as we piled into the open-air Jeep, bundled up with blankets on our laps and jackets zipped up to our chins, we—me, Barb, and another dozen or so passengers—were encouraged not to feel hopeful, that there hadn't been a tiger sighting in days. Although this Rajasthani preserve was known for its tiger population, it was not a zoo. We were certain to see plenty of wildlife, but as far as getting to see the main attraction—the Bengal tiger—there were no guarantees. This felt like a fair exchange. As a guest in the tiger's habitat, I might not get to see one, but at least I'd go home knowing the tigers weren't sighted because they were *free* and simply happened to be roaming about in areas we didn't visit that day. It wasn't personal.

We entered the park through a moss-covered stone entryway, which made me feel for a moment like I was passing through the remnants of a long-ago civilization taken over by the uninhibited growth of flora and foliage. We were instructed to remain in the Jeep at all times as we drove into the reserve and settled in for our tour.

We exchanged quiet chit-chat at first, but our soundtrack eventually turned exclusively to the motor of the Jeep, its gears shifting up and down as we made our way along sharp curves and elevations. The langur monkeys were out and about, as were the sambar deer and myna birds. With Barb sitting behind me, I got into the habit of silently pointing out any animal I saw rather than turning around and exclaiming, "Look!"— another one of my tiny routines that Barb found amusing.

No other Jeeps or buses traveled with us, but our trackers remained in constant communication with other guides around the park on walkie-talkies, everyone keeping each other updated on the signs that indicated a tiger on the prowl: paw prints, sightings, and the nervous titter of other wildlife. Over the next few hours, we didn't find any tigers, but it was fascinating to watch our guides work, the way they gathered clues from the movement of branches and, when we were situated near the edge of a bluff overlooking a forested valley, from the sounds traveling beneath the tree canopy. We sat quietly as they observed and listened. After a few minutes, they confirmed there was commotion afoot, and we headed in a new direction. We met another guide down the road who mentioned nearby paw tracks, and we took a few detours based on his data.

We drove slowly for another few miles on the bumpy dirt road until our guides informed us we had to make our way back to the entrance of the park. It was disappointing that our time in the park had to wind down just as it seemed we were figuring out the tiger's whereabouts, but everyone was in good spirits nonetheless.

When we'd entered the park earlier that morning, we passed a small body of water that held the promise of a possible crocodile sighting. Since we hadn't seen one at the beginning of our ride, our guides decided to take us back the same way, hopeful one might be out of the water and sunbathing by then. The landscape was bright and glittery, a change from the misty gray of early morning. The day was past its phase of waking up and now pulsed, energized and alive. I pushed the blanket off my lap and unzipped my windbreaker, happy to feel the sun's warmth on my face.

I scanned the shoreline as our Jeep plodded along, the water sparkling in the sunlight, and something I was not expecting—something none of us, even our guides, were expecting—came into view. Once my brain caught up with my eyes, I realized I was looking at a full-grown tiger, and it was walking straight toward us. As it approached, it gave our Jeep a calm, fixed stare, and I immediately, surprisingly, started crying. My reverie was broken by the reaction of our guides. Even though they were experienced trackers who had cataloged countless tiger sightings, their exuberance was like a champagne cork popping out of the bottle.

"*This* is magic moment!" the driver exclaimed with a hand raised in the air as if in exalted prayer. "This is *magic moment!*"

I looked at him and saw my own reflection: mouth agape, tears in eyes. This alone was a revelation—that none of us need be immune to life's wonders, even if they were, to us, commonplace. How many tigers had our guide seen here in Ranthambore? I had no idea. No matter the number, he saw that moment as a miracle. In that instant I knew, body and soul, he was right: this *was* a magic moment.

As the tiger walked toward us, our driver reversed and pulled up to a small hill just off the road. For a blissful ten minutes, we had front-row seats to the tiger's quiet meanderings. We watched him walk toward the water and sprawl out on the ground before offering us a big, gaping yawn, perhaps to let us know our presence in his home couldn't possibly have bored him more. We were guests in his domain, so we sat quietly and watched him, the *click-click-click* of cameras in the background.

After taking a few photos myself, I set mine down, wanting to watch him with my own eyes, rather than through a viewfinder, for as long as possible. When I turned around to look at Barb, I saw she had been crying too.

We cried quite a few times on that trip—at the sight of other animals, at the kindness of strangers, out of exhaustion and overwhelm. We laughed and sobbed and whooped and prayed, letting all the emotions flow through us—day by day, moment by moment. In order to fully experience all the beauty and wonder India had to offer, we knew we had to be open to all of its challenges as well—the poverty, the crowds, the noise. We went home filled in ways we hadn't expected and having received gifts we hadn't seen coming, just like the tiger who emerged, seemingly out of nowhere, right in front of our Jeep on a cold, misty morning in Ranthambore.

It wasn't just the tiger that caught my breath. It was his wildness—that untamed, unqualified ferocity that kept his heart pumping and drove his will to survive. The moment I saw him, I received another clue as to how and why India is able to draw me in, hold me rapt, and send me home wanting more. India is modern and sophisticated, and it is also *wild*. It has the power to surprise, the ability to stun. It wakes me up in a way no other part of the world has even come close to doing.

Every place I've traveled has left a unique impression on me, has somehow altered my view of the world and my place in it, but India's mark has made the deepest impression. Even though I am the one who came to India, it is India that came swinging into me, smashing down walls I didn't even know existed, shining light on sensitivities—and strengths—I didn't know I had. Like the tiger that elicited a tidal wave of emotion in Ranthambore four years ago, India, once again, has swept me off my feet this year and showed me what it means to step boldly out into the world, into the blinding light of the unknown.

GLOSSARY

Aarti: a Hindu ritual of worship in which light from wicks soaked in ghee (purified butter) or camphor is offered to one or more deities

Agra: a city in northern India, home to the Taj Mahal

Bindi: a colored dot worn on the forehead, at times as adornment, at other times to represent the third eye

Buddhism: the world's fourth largest religion, based on the original teachings of the Buddha

Chai: a type of Indian tea, made especially by boiling the tea leaves with milk, sugar, and cardamom (see recipe on page 133)

Delhi: the capital of India, with a population of more than 11 million

Deogarh: prounounced dee-oh-gar, a small city in Rajasthan

Diya: an oil lamp or candle, used mainly in India and Nepal, for religious purposes

Doms: "Hindu's undertakers," who assist families with cremation rituals, most especially in Varanasi

Garam masala: a spice mix popular in northern India made with cardamom, cinnamon, cloves, cumin, black pepper, and coriander

Ghat: a flight of steps leading down to a river

Guru: a Hindu or Buddhist spiritual teacher

Hinduism: an Indian religion and dharma, or a way of life, called the oldest religion in the world

Jainism: a nontheistic religion that teaches salvation by perfection through successive lives and noninjury to living creatures

Jaipur: the capital of Rajasthan, known as "the Pink City"

Kirtan: a Sanskrit word that means narrating, reciting, telling, describing an idea or story; also refers to a musical religious performance

Langar: the term used in Sikhism for the community kitchen where a free meal is served to all the visitors without distinction of religion, caste, gender, economic status, or ethnicity

Makar Sankranti: a festival day in the Hindu calendar marking the first day of sun's transit into the winter solstice

Moksha: the release from the cycle of rebirth impelled by the law of karma in Hinduism and Jainism

Namaste: a gesture of greeting in India with hands held together in the prayer position at one's heart, literally translated to mean *I bow to you*

Qawwali: a style of Sufi devotional music popular in south Asia

Rajasthan: India's largest state, which shares a border with Pakistan

Sadhu: a holy man, sage, or ascetic

Samode: a village forty-two kilometers from Jaipur, famous for its fort and *haveli* (mansion)

Samsara: the cycle of death and rebirth to which life in the material world is bound, in Hinduism and Buddhism

Shalwar kameez: a long tunic worn over a pair of baggy trousers, usually by women

Sikhism: a monotheistic religion that originated in India; the fifth-largest and one of the youngest of the major world religions

Sufism: a mystical Islamic belief and practice in which Muslims seek to find the truth of divine love and knowledge through direct personal experience of God

Tabla: a pair of small hand drums attached together, used in Indian music

Uttar Pradesh: a state in northern India bordering Nepal

Varanasi: a city in the northern Indian state of Uttar Pradesh dating to the 11th century BC and regarded as the spiritual capital of India

BIBLIOGRAPHY + RECOMMENDED RESOURCES

Shantaram by Gregory David Roberts

Nine Lives: In Search of the Sacred in Modern India by William Dalrymple

Hindu Rites and Rituals by K. V. Singh

Chai Pilgrimage by Patrick Shaw and Jenny Kostecki-Shaw

Tales by Light, Season 2, Episode 5, "Life and Death: Part 1" (Netflix)

Slumdog Millionaire (film)

The Lunchbox (film)

Lion (film)

The Elements Trilogy by Deepa Mehta (films)

The Darjeeling Limited (film)

The Best Exotic Marigold Hotel (film)

GRATITUDE

Thank you, Barb Skoog, for being brave enough to go to India with me in 2014, even after you saw the list I made of all the ways I'm crazy. Thank you, Kolleen Harrison and Jennette Nielsen, for trusting Barb and me enough to join us on our second trip there in 2018. Thank you to all four of you for making sure I never twisted my ankle, always had water, and wasn't without tissues. Thank you for being such kind, gracious, patient, loving women and travel companions. I'd go anywhere in the world with you.

Thank you, Vineeta Nair and Nisha Sampath, for showing me what it means to walk the path of love, devotion, and beauty. The miles between us do nothing to dim the light I see in you.

Thank you, Enchanting Travels, for creating such inspiring journeys in India. Many thanks to all of our tour guides and drivers, most especially Dinesh Tiwari in Varanasi and Vikram Singh in Jaipur.

Thank you, Jen Gray, Pixie Lighthorse, Michelle Madden-Smith, and Melody Ross, for keeping the fires at home burning for the four of us. I felt your love every step of the way.

To Melissa Piccola, Johnny and Nancy Faulkner, David Davis, Jill and Will Rivera, Alex and Laurette Johnston, Mark and Cheri Swank, Heidi Whitney, Kellen Brugman, Eric Smith, Karen Jørgenson, the Rocha Family, Lisa Field, Anne Carmack, Blair Beggan, Lisa Occhipinti, Jen Lee, Tom and Sally Poelzer, Shannon Jackson Arnold, and Stephanie Sharp: Your love and support carried me all the way from Southern California to a new life in the Midwest. Without you, none of it would have been possible. Thank you.

Thank you, Liz Kalloch, Maya Stein, Amy Tingle, Grace Moore, Stefanie Renee, Danielle Spiewak, and Jonatha Brooke, for your wild beauty, magnificent humor, and enduring love.

Thank you, Mari Robeson and Kimberly Wilson, for always shining such a bright light of encouragement no matter what I'm doing. Your steady presence through my life and work has been a tremendous source of joy.

Thank you, Meredith Klein, for contributing your delicious recipes.

Thank you, Christianne Squires, for, once again, smoothing down the rough edges of my writing with such skill, wisdom, and kindness. Working with you is a dream, and I'm never letting you go—both as my editor and my friend.

Thank you to my family for providing all the things I need most in the world—love, grace, beauty, kindness, laughter, compassion, and forgiveness. Words cannot express how grateful I am that the stars aligned in such a way that I've ended up walking through this world with you by my side. I love you forever.

Thank you, Lawrence. I love that you hate it when I leave home but encourage me to travel anyway. I love that you hate it when I leave home. I love that the most exquisite moment of any trip I take is the day I return home—to you, our life, and our adventures.

CPSIA information can be obtained
at www.ICGtesting.com
Printed in the USA
LVHW071018211120
672147LV00012BA/294